S0-BEZ-020

REDS

The Second Greatest Generation

Rebecca
all the best wishes
to you!

Joseph Romano

JOSEPH J ROMANO

Copyright © 2018 Joseph J Romano
All rights reserved
First Edition

PAGE PUBLISHING, INC.
New York, NY

First originally published by Page Publishing, Inc. 2018

ISBN 978-1-64214-668-4 (Paperback)
ISBN 978-1-64214-669-1 (Digital)

Printed in the United States of America

Acknowledgments

The philosopher R. G. Collingwood rightfully asserts that every attempt at an aesthetic work demands the collaboration of many people. He eschews the notion of the lonely painter or writer hidden away in his secret lair, claiming no help or contact with anyone except his muses. In Collingwood's view, art reveals reality rather than conceals it behind a pretentious mystique of truths known only by the author.

Whether this story about some ordinary boys deserves the merits of art is for a collaborative reader to judge. While not claiming any special muses, this author acknowledges the important collaboration of many people. The telling of this story would not have been enjoyable for me or possible without the people in my life who made it possible.

My wife, Jeanne, who critiqued many of the ideas in the story, evaluating their universal worth; my sister, Margaret, who shared similar experiences in the small town of our youth; my late and beloved brother, Fran, who critiqued the early parts of the book before leaving us. The boys and girls I grew up with as together we learned the lessons of life.

My many teachers who taught me that knowledge was lovable in and of itself, that learning was as natural and nutritious as eating—and maybe a little more important.

My many students who continue to challenge me to ponder the important questions of life, hopefully with humor and wit and as little of self-importance as possible.

My special gratitude is to Stan Thompson who edited and produced the audio version of this work. Stan worked tirelessly on the studio recording, and I am deeply grateful for his patience and expertise.

Thanks to Steve Highsmith, who graciously lent his wonderful talent as the voice of Billy's Notebook. Steve also made invaluable editing contributions.

Also, thanks to Courtney O'Connor and Belinda Thresher, whose editing advice and inspiring message are greatly appreciated

Finally, thanks to Jeff Gingrich, the Provost of Cabrini University, who supported the final production.

Prologue

The telling of this story began several years ago when the author was invited to participate in a panel discussion at Cabrini University. The student philosophy club had invited him and three other professors to offer their views on the current status of organized play for kids. The event may have been prompted by reports of loud and somewhat obnoxious parents at their kid's soccer or little league baseball games. The panel members were not given specific guidelines other than engendering discussion from the student-audience who would attend. They could offer favorable opinions, negative ones, or simply present some pro-and-con remarks relevant to the topic of structured play of children.

Wanting to offer something other than a lecture-type talk that might remind the student-audience of a classroom, the author decided to tell a story about five boys growing up in a blue-collar town in the 1940s and early 1950s. The boys, with no adult supervision, organized a neighborhood baseball team along with three other teams from the same small town.

The students responded favorably to his story of Reds and his buddies forming a league of their own without any adult intervention—or even knowledge. They appreciated how the kids of this early generation learned responsibility on their own—basically from within. How natural leadership emerged from the social interaction of the youngsters, and how values were learned and internalized as part of their life experiences.

The story told that evening grew into the present production, as events were recalled that were transformative before that term became popular. Those who reflected on this period of change began to appreciate how that older generation learned with an unvarnished simplicity, the profound lessons of life.

It is mostly a true story, although with enough creative interchanging of names, places, and events that would make it qualify as a creative nonfictional work. What it is called is not nearly as important as what it says. It is an ode to youth. That time when kids are not yet molded to the conformity of social conventions. Not that all social conventions are bad.

And of course, that is the point of the story. How and when do we learn what social norms are favorable for happiness—and should be sustained from generation to generation, and which are stereo-typically stunting of individuals living in that society and should be rejected?

The youngsters in the story relied more on an internal feel for doing the right thing, at the right time. They did not need the adults of society to tell them how to be fair and not to cheat when they played their ballgames, how to relate to other kids of different religions or races.

Values change, people change, societies change. This story will not appeal to those who prefer rote answers to profound questions or prefer a more-absolutistic approach to life. The lives of these boys of the mid-twentieth century was no more simple or complex than any other generation. We all live in the same reality—and yet in many ways, it is different and unique to each one of us. The "same but different" paradox threads its way through the story. Hopefully, their lives will shed some small light on the "same generational differ-ences" each age faces, without unduly stereotyping each generation. So many books offer simple characteristics marking off certain dates and traits with categorical certainty and then filling in the gaps with anecdotal information in the disguise of facts. So we have the baby boomers and the "generation X" gang, the millennials, and now gen-eration Z.

The one deserving branding of any generation is the name "The Greatest Generation," which Tom Brokaw so adequately bestowed on those brave people who faced down two catastrophic events of the twentieth century—the Great Depression and World War II. It is suggested here that boys of this story deserve the title "Second Greatest Generation." They experienced the same fears and anxieties of their brave parents but without the power of direct involvement.

The narrative shapes the major social issues of then—and now, around the lives of these boys as they grow up in a world devastated by threats to life itself through poverty and warfare. Economic divisions of rich and poor, insufferable racial discrimination, the pollution of the river they fished in and of the air they breathed, rejection of same-sex desires by the heterosexual majority—these are some of the societal realities encountered by these youngsters who ostensibly wanted nothing more than to play baseball on their own neighborhood team. They do more than that, however, as their lives reflect many of those social challenges that remain with us today.

They reflect an honesty of youth as they attend their public school, practice their received faith, go to the movies, take camping trips, meet girls, and play baseball in their own home-made league. There is a sincere simplicity in the responses to life's trials from those whose lives have not yet been poured into the social molds of conformity and predictability. In their innocence in carrying out their daily tasks, one can see a profound difference between how the boys value the lessons of life from that of their adult counterparts. Their lived experiences have greater meaning and contain immeasurable lessons than ever imagined by the very adults with whom they are in daily contact.

The subtle but striking difference between the openness of youth and the limiting conformity of adult life is a recurring theme—whether the experiences are joyful or sorrowful. The lives of the young embrace the basic dichotomy of comedy and tragedy, of laughing and crying. In attaining adulthood, these youngsters preserved this un-nuanced approach to life as a mark of true maturity—at any age.

Their lives are a revelation of universal truths about these joys and sorrows of life that are just beneath the threshold of their consciousness and have long been submerged and forgotten by most adults. It is the boys' uncomplicated immersion in life that sustains the innocence of their youth even as they grow old. Their lives become paradigms of a deeper search for meaning, narrated as philosophical points of view on economics, politics, love and gender relationships, aging, and mortality.

It is hoped that their lives give voice to commonly held aspirations that transcend time, place, and generations.

Chapter One

Reds

This is the story of the Sixth Avenue Wildcats. A neighborhood sandlot baseball team organized, staffed, and funded by the boys who lived on Sixth Avenue in a small steel mill town hugging a river about fifteen miles west of Philadelphia. These ninth, tenth, and eleventh grade boys loved baseball and played on a field that they sometimes shared with some milk cows owned by Mr. Januzelli.

The boys loved baseball and gravitated together by the mere proximity of their row houses on Sixth Avenue. They collected and sold old newspapers, rags, and scrap metal and purchased plain white T-shirts and some paper alphabet decals—the kind your mom can iron on the front of your shirt. These were the formal "uniforms" of the Wildcats, worn only on game days and never at practice. The main organizer and natural leader of the Wildcats was a tall, skinny kid named Reds. If this team had been located in New York City, he would have been called "Red," but this was southeastern Pennsylvania and he was called "Reds."

Reds was a quiet but effective leader who invited the neighborhood boys—all of them of an appropriate age—to join the team. He contacted boys from other parts of the town who had organized similar teams made up of kids the same ages. There was the Third Avenue Bulldogs, the Spring Mill Avenue Blue Jays, and the Ninth Avenue Cardinals. A schedule was mutually agreed upon for the summer months and an equitable distribution of home and away games decided upon by the respective unofficial leaders of the various teams. Away games presented no problem for any of the teams since the town was small enough so that any field was within easy bicycle pedaling from any team's neighborhood.

It was mentioned that Reds was the leader of the Wildcats and one wonders how he got to hold that enviable position. He certainly wasn't elected by any vote of the other boys, nor was he appointed by any adult. In fact, not many of the parents knew about the inner workings of the team's organization—except perhaps the ironing work that the moms performed. The parents certainly knew that their boys were playing baseball, but other than that, it was purely a kids' venture from top to bottom.

It was solely on the strength of Reds's even-tempered and fair-minded persona that the mantle of "leader" fell on him. He was a little older than most of the other boys, but only by a few months at most. There were a few older boys—Ernie, to mention one—who no right-thinking kid would imagine to be capable of doing what Reds seem to do effortlessly. To organize the team, plan how to earn money for shirts and balls and bats, to contact other teams and plan a schedule, to evaluate talent and get the right player in the right position. Reds did all of this without breaking a sweat, as the kids were wont to say.

Reds knew, for example, that speedy Billy could run down any fly ball hit within two miles of centerfield and that his speed and keen eye at the plate made him the perfect leadoff man. Billy rarely swung at anything outside the strike zone, never struck out, and drew many a base-on balls. Billy could control the bat as well. As a right-handed batter, he could punch the ball to right field, behind the base runner on a hit-and-run play, or pull it down the line over the third baseman's head. Nobody taught Billy to do this. He never went to any baseball camp—none of the boys did. They learned how to play the game by simply *playing* the game. Reds knew what Billy could do and his lineup had Billy leading off and playing center field.

Reds was that kind of leader that when a long shot went soaring to dead center field, Reds would calmly call out from his short stop position, "You got it, Billy." Such confidence in his players from a natural leader! And more often than not, Billy ran down the ball. In fact, there was one game against Spring Mill, when big Bill Crawford, the clean-up hitter for the Blue Jays, hit an immense drive to dead center. Billy, who always played a shallow center field, turned at the crack of the bat and raced along the trajectory of the ball and, with his back to the infield, looked up at the right moment and made an over-the-shoulder catch. On a smaller scale, it was the exact kind of catch that Willy Mays made against Vic Wertz in that well-known series game pitting the New York Giants against the Detroit Tigers. "Nice catch, Billy," Reds said quietly.

"Way to go, Billy," said Big Joe from first base.

"Atta boy, Billy," called Ernie from his catching position behind the plate. No big deal. No cheering crowds. No expectations of glory or rewards or adult praise. They were kids playing ball. And they were having fun.

Lest you think that this is some kind of kid's utopia in baseball land, know that there were issues. Gussie, for example was not always happy playing right field. He was smart enough to know that right field in a baseball world, where most players were right-handed, was not the most active position on the field. He also knew that when teams could only field eight players, right field was considered foul ball territory. Gussie was not exactly a dimwit. "C'mon, Reds, how come I always play out here?" he called one day from his lonely position.

"Okay, Gussie," answered Reds, "one more inning, then we can switch. I'll play right, and you can take over at short stop. Okay?"

"Gee, thanks, Reds," Gussie gushed with gratitude." See what a leader Reds was! Now granted it was also the bottom of the seventh and the Wildcats were leading 11–1. But that's okay. Reds did not have to do that. He just knew how to establish right relations among his players—and he was just a kid himself. He was exemplary in employing best practices of leadership in sandlot baseball.

Then there was Ernie. Ernie was a large boy. A very large boy and he was the catcher on the Wildcats team. Ernie used his generous size to his advantage. He could hit the ball a mile. He struck out a lot, but Reds had him batting in the bottom of the order and put him in position to drive in a lot of runs even if he did not score often. Ernie would scorch the ball deep to the outfield and never make it past first base. If they kept records in this homemade kids' league—which of course they did not—Ernie would have held the record for the number of longest singles in the league. He could hit, but he just could not run.

One game he drove a ball deep into the left-center field gap. It was an awesome shot that drew the attention of the kids on both teams especially the outfielders who were trekking after the ball. When everyone's attention refocused on Ernie, he was just reaching first base. In addition to his slowness afoot, Ernie, on this occasion, was having trouble with his low-hanging trousers, and he was trying to run and hold up his pants at the same time. Midway between first and second, gravity prevailed over lift, and Ernie's pants slid down to his ankles, tripping the rotund catcher who fell to the turf with a seismic thud. He would have gotten a perfect ten for swan diving in an aquatic meet. The ball, in the meantime, was returned to the infield where the second baseman ceremoniously tagged Ernie out by applying the ball where Plumbers have no shame. Ernie, once again, would have recorded a very long single.

What happened next is more important than a kids' baseball game. The still shot of Ernie on the ground and the second baseman over him frozen in a comic tableau was broken by the trembling of Ernie's body—a quiver, a shaking, a rumbling, and a sudden burst of uproaring laughter from the fallen catcher. Ernie was laughing so hard he couldn't get up. Then the second baseman, then all the rest of the players—both teams howling with side-splitting laughter that held up the game for fifteen minutes. The very bottom half of that same inning, Ernie threw out two of the Bulldog runners trying to steal second with perfect pegs to the second base bag.

"Way to go, Ernie."

"Nice peg, Ernie."

Most of the games the Wildcats played ended the same way. The kids on the other team would go pedaling off toward their homes and the Wildcats would wind up horsing around as kids usually do—punching arms, wrestling around in the grass, inventing new unflattering nicknames for each other. They eventually would wind up at Jesse's soda fountain where they would gorge themselves on gigantic milkshakes. They never seemed to care if they won or lost the game. But don't kid yourself. They had fun. Also, don't ever doubt that they took their play seriously. *They* earned the money for their meager equipment. *They* thought up their own team name and style of uniform. *They* knew how to affix a screw to a broken bat so that they would not have to buy a new one. They repaired old baseballs with black electrical tape. They settled their own arguments and laughed, not cried, over their mistakes. They challenged their own good judgments by serving as umpires when their team was at bat. Standing behind the pitcher and calling balls and strikes for both teams was a supreme test of impartiality and fairness. They were kids learning on their own how to make adult decisions. They were *internalizing* values that their parents could only present *externally* to them. They were kids with a purpose, and it was a kid's purpose. And they were having fun.

Chapter Two

Buy Me Some Peanuts and Crackerjack

About three or four times during the lazy hazy days of summer, several of the Sixth Avenue gang would walk the four blocks or so down to the train station on the edge of the Schuylkill River and get the Pennsylvania line to North Broad Street in Philadelphia. Their destination was old Shibe Park at Twenty-First and Lehigh Avenue where, on most summer Sundays, there was a double-header baseball ball game featuring either the Philadelphia Athletics of the American League or the Phillies who represented one of the oldest franchises in the national league—lovingly referred to then as the senior circuit.

Mothers dutifully packed lunches for the boys—usually peanut butter and jelly sandwiches on soft, tasteless white "American" bread, which indicated that the outing was not important enough to merit the crusty and tasty Italian bread baked in the outdoor brick ovens of Mrs. Ianucci. This generous neighbor baked once a week, flooding the neighborhood with celestial scents of brick oven-baked bread, which she routinely offered to the neighborhood kids. She also provided a vat of sweet cream butter, which the youngsters troweled onto the bread, creating a combination taste of freshly baked dough in a hardened brown crust made complete with the sweet butter. Tastes such as this do not come often in one's lifetime. Freshly baked Italian bread from an outdoor brick oven. This explains the somewhat contemptuous expression, among Italian immigrant families, "American bread," which had nothing to do with one's political opinion of one's new life in America, but had everything to do with a taste test comparison between Mrs. Iannuci's culinary accomplishments and the soft, mushy, tasteless, and square white bread mass produced by the Bond Baking company. The first-generation American kids inherited this expression from their immigrant parents who seemed to pass the unflattering remark along with their genes. The boys of the Wildcat team mostly used the tasteless concoction to bait their fishing hooks when they fished in the Schuylkill River for carp and catfish. The white bread sandwiches were a stop gap measure until hot dogs could be scarfed down at the doubleheaders on Sundays.

The thirty-minute train ride to North Philadelphia always proved to be an eventful occasion, beginning with the wary glances of a suspicious conductor. Five or six early-teen energetic boys seemed an unruly group to any thinking adult, let alone a uniformed authority figure charged with maintaining order on a moving train. The fact is that the aptly named Wildcats had a hard time staying in their seats.

Then there was the time that Ernie had to "go to the bathroom," which was at the front of the car and had a door that was impeded by the main door to the car in which the boys were riding. Whenever the train stopped—it was a local train with many stops—the conductor would enter the car and push the door back in a locked position against the restroom door as he called out the appropriate station. Seconds after the conductor had fastened the door, Ernie opened the lavatory door and came face-to-face with *another door*—the main car door that completely blocked the restroom exit, trapping Ernie in the restroom.

So there was Ernie with this goofy grin on his face, nose against the second glass door, surprised that he was trapped in the restroom. The conductor did not appreciate the howls and hoots that came from the boys as they saw Ernie's contorted face pressed against the glass door. Now understand that the boys were not bad kids—not at all. They were kids who eventually grew into manhood, and each became solid members of the small town in which they were born. They settled down, got jobs— mostly in the factories and mills nearby, married local girls, had kids of their own, got their own mortgaged homes, and grew old. No adult, especially not the conductor, could appreciate the humor they saw in that train incident. And maybe that is a shame.

Maybe if they had been that conductor, they too would have been perturbed by the raucous reaction of the boys at the comic scene. Maybe civilized society knocks the silliness out of youngsters. But maybe it knocks something else out as well. And maybe that is too bad. Perhaps structured society takes from them spontaneity and creativity and ingenuity—the same creativeness that prompted them to form their own baseball league designed and played under their terms. Perhaps as adults, they will never have that same carefree existence that comes so authentically from deep inside. Social structure demands conformity from without; the boys experienced a conformity to their own feelings and desires within. And that may not be so bad.

The boys quieted down, the train moved on, and Ernie escaped from his prison johnnie. What they desired now was to get to the ball park and watch a doubleheader. The Phillies were playing today, and if they got there early, they might catch a few players going into the players' entrance at the side of old Shibe Park.

When the train arrived at the North Broad Street terminal, the boys eschewed the steps leading down from the platform and tumbled down a steep grassy bank along a well-worn shortcut to the street below. They reveled in this quick path leading to Twenty-First and Lehigh Avenue, which allowed them to beat other park goers to the ticket gates. Anyway, before purchasing their left field bleacher seats, they wanted to hang out at the players' entrance. They were plenty early to catch a few players, and sure enough, after a few minutes hanging out on the sidewalk, two Phillies players came sauntering around the corner heading for the players' entrance. One player was immediately recognized for his height. It was the pitcher 'Schoolboy" Rowe himself, a six-foot, four-inch mountain of a man who towered over the boys who were in awe that they were face-to-face with what had only been an image on a baseball card. *Lynwood Thomas "Schoolboy" Rowe; Waco, Texas; bats right; throws right; pitcher.* And here was the baseball card alive and in person smiling at the Sixth Avenue Wildcats. Only Big Joe had the presence to mumble, "Hey, Schoolboy, hit a homer for us." We all knew that Schoolboy was one of the best pinch hitters the Phils had when he wasn't pitching, and he had indeed hit a few homers in that pinch hit role. No one else said a word; no one asked for an autograph. In a matter of seconds, the meeting was over and Rowe disappeared through the door.

"Did you see that!" Gussie gushed.

"I told you we would see a player," chimed in Billy.

The gang walked excitedly toward the left field entrance, pushing and shoving each other with make-believe Schoolboy Rowe pitching moves and talking excitedly about the great experience of encountering a real player.

Doubleheaders are long. Some speculate that baseball eliminated the two-for-the-price-of-one deal for economic reasons, but others will argue that the psychology of one's attention span is just as important a reason for abandoning them. The focus that the fans had on the game being played on the field was inversely proportionate to the detritus that littered the field below the left field stands. By the fifth inning of the second game, the left fielder would have to search for any ball bouncing around in the corner. Sandwich wrappers, programs, model airplanes made out of scrap paper—all found their way out of the stands and onto the field, burying the left fielder in a blizzard of waste.

There was another factor that may have accounted for a bit of disinterest in the games. In the mid-1940s, the Phillies were not a very good team. There were only eight teams in each league then—the American and National Leagues. The winners in each league played each other at the end of the season in the World Series—end of story. Baseball's business moguls had not yet figured out the profit motive of extending the schedule to include many more games and adding a contrived playoff system, allowing more teams to participate in "post-season play." In addition to yielding more revenue for the clubs, the new system would generate greater fan interest with the hope that their second or third place team might still "make the playoffs" and extend the season. Most teams under the old system found themselves eliminated from World Series play well before the season ended. This was the case of the Phillies laboring to complete that doubleheader in the mid-1940s. It must be confessed, however, that while the adult fans might lose interest in games that "might not mean anything," this was not true of the youngsters. Again, a generation gap reveals an interest on the part of the kids that is beyond scores, standings, and wins and losses. They liked the game itself so that the scores or standings were not of great significance. The boys usually stayed until the bitter end—happy when the home team won, indifferent when they lost, and always greatly appreciative of seeing professional baseball played and having models to emulate when they turned their own double plays or hit-and-run strategy.

There was another reason for waiting out both games. There was always the enticing hope that a player—hopefully a hometowner—would belt a ball into the left field stands and some lucky kid would have a treasured souvenir. Sometimes the games were mercifully ended, or suspended, by the Pennsylvania Blue Laws which prohibited sporting events to extend beyond a certain time on Sunday lest the games would interfere with evening church services. God forbid that sports should interfere with faith—literally. These two games went quickly, however, with no need for holier-than-thou Blue Laws to violate either the first amendment or the sacred game of baseball. The quickness of the games was in part due to the inept play of the Phillies who scored few runs and succumbed to the lowly Cubs in both ends of the doubleheader.

The boy's endurance in seeing the games to the end paid off beyond their wildest expectations. Schoolboy Rowe did pinch hit in the bottom of the eighth inning and hit a deep fly to left causing a brief moment of excitement from the few remaining fans. The ball was caught on the warning track and simply resulted in a long out. In the bottom of the ninth, however, with the game already a lost cause, Del Ennis, the hometown rookie slugger, crushed a mammoth home run that struck the front railing of the left field upper deck. The ball spun forward off the railing and catapulted over ten rows of empty seats, landing one row below the seats occupied by Reds and the Wildcat gang. Quick and nimble, Billy leapt over the seats in front and trapped the spinning ball against the back cement. Hallelujah! Heaven on earth! Joy and Rapture! How many people go to countless games hoping against hope, gloves at the ready, and never come close to capturing a treasured baseball souvenir. "Way to go, Billy," said Reds with a smile.

"Nice grab, Bill," said Big Joe. And now, here was Billy, grinning from ear to ear with a face lit up like Moses coming down from Mount Sinai. His Wildcat teammates were going crazy. Not only an official National League baseball from a real game, but a home run ball—not a mere foul ball. And not any old home run, but off the bat of Del Ennis, one who would enhance the value of the ball by becoming a genuine all-star player who would lead the Phillies to a World Series against the Yankees four years later.

The boys didn't know this, of course, and let it be noted that after several weeks of exhibiting the ball in various school classrooms and sandlot fields, they eventually used the ball (a little dirty now by much handling) in one of their own games. What other kids could say that they used a real major league ball in their own game. Adults would not see it that way. In fact, Billy's dad really laid into him when he learned that the ball had been used in one of their games and was now "ruined" and devoid of any sports memorabilia value. "Why did you do a dumb thing like that," he growled. "Don't you know that in twenty years or so that ball would have been worth a lot of money!"

Is it that adults just don't get it? Kids don't care about the future value of memorabilia. They don't have memorabilia. They traded, swapped, and played with their precious baseballs cards as well. They didn't wrap them carefully in saran wrap and store them away waiting for their market value to kick in. They were baseball cards—for kids. If any contrived value accrued from cheaply made cards packaged with fleers bubblegum, it was not a kid's commercial scheme. Kids have their own simple and honest value system. There is nothing contrived or fake about it

At any rate, Billy would survive his father's rant about "destroying a valuable memorabilia." And the kids really did enjoy playing with that special ball. When they eventually knocked the cover off, they re-covered it with black electrical tape and continued using it much to the chagrin of Billy's father.

But now they were trudging back to the train station, tired but happy, walking at a slow gait markedly different from their excited exit from the train to the ball park earlier that day. They walked up the concrete walk instead of scrambling up the steep sloped shortcut, boarded the train, and slumped in their seats. They had seen a doubleheader. They were tired but content. The conductor would have no cause for concern regarding their behavior on the trip home. And Ernie did not have to go to the restroom.

Chapter Three

Parallel Worlds: One White, One Black

T he boys of the sandlot Wildcats lived on the three blocks of Sixth Avenue that ran from the main street of town to the dead-end wall of the abandoned stone quarry. Most of the homes of those three blocks, with the exception of a few old single homes, were called at that time "row homes." Much later, under the soothing hand of real estate brokers, they would be renamed "town-houses." The homes were old, but sturdy, made of cement block with generous front porches where neighbors sat on rockers and minded everyone's business. Billy lived on the third block a few homes away from the stone wall that sealed off the quarry, which was now used as one of the town's unofficial waste sites. Part of the wages that Billy and his teammates earned to buy the scant equipment for their team came from weekly trips down the back alley and around to the site where they dumped their neighbors trash for twenty-five cents a wagonload.

On Billy's north side of the three hundred blocks, there were no single homes—rather, a long straight row of houses, all with continuous porch roofs attached so that one could climb out the front bedroom window of the end house and walk unimpeded across the entire roof line to the house at other end of the row.

In fact, one hot summer evening, well after midnight, Billy's dad was aroused from a fitful sleep, by a fight between a father and his teenage daughter, who lived at the opposite end of the row from Billy's. The daughter, to make a point in the dispute, had climbed on to the roof and walked the entire length, arguing with her angry dad who was on the pavement below, following her path and shouting up to her as loudly as she bellowed back at him. It was truly a Kafkaesque scene in which the outraged daughter threatened to jump off the roof if her father did not accede to her teenage wishes. Billy's dad, angry at having his sleep interrupted when the sweltering hot night was impediment enough to a good night's sleep, went to his open front window and yelled, "For Chris's sake, if you're going to kill yourself, go down to your own goddam roof and jump!" Such was life on the three hundredth block of Sixth Avenue.

It was an ethnically mixed block, with Italian and Poles living on the north side of the street; and a few Irish, Italian, and families of unknown ethnicity on the other side, where there was also a small cluster of three row homes occupied by black families. Most of the African American families lived on the east end of town on a street adjacent to the river. They clustered around their church, the African Methodist Episcopal Church. It was common in small-town America to gain social comfort within the confines of one's ethnic and religious community. Just as Irish, Italian, and Polish immigrants huddled around the churches built by their own labors, so the blacks did as well. Churches were the glue that held together those who would otherwise be blown away by the winds of social indifference or prejudice. This was especially necessary for blacks who, unlike their counterparts, the lower-class immigrants from Europe, could not easily blend into society after a generation or two. Through inter-ethnic marriage, access to political power, and labor unions, the ethnic Irish, Polish, and Italians of the town could climb the social ladder of respectability.

The three black families living across the street from Billy's row home were an anomaly to the white immigrant families living alongside and across the street from them. They belonged to the AME Church that was on the other side of town and spent most of their time out of their homes with their friends and relatives in the "negro" part of town. They were renting on Sixth Avenue, seemed to be related to each other, and were very friendly and cordial on those rare occasions they appeared outside. However, they never bought food where the other neighbors shopped for groceries and were rarely seen in the three-block shopping district of town. If they went to the local movie house, they sat far off in a side section separated from the main seating section, where all the black folks of town sat when attending the theater. In the world they lived in, there was a separate and parallel engagement with all the cultural activities that occupied the lives of the people in that town. Churches, grocery stores, beauty parlors, barber shops, recreational swimming, and amusement parks were all in the infamous words of seven Supreme Court justices, "separate but equal."

The one exception—in a way—was the public school, which the few African American students attended and readily engaged the other kids in the daily duties imposed by educational standards. While many close friendships were forged between blacks and whites at the local public school, these relationships did not really extend beyond the walls of the school. At the end of the school day, the two groups went their respective ways.

The family in the middle of the three homes had two boys. Jayroy was the same age as Billy and most of the other members of the Wildcat team. Jayroy had a younger brother, William, who often tagged after his older brother, and sometimes played catch on the front pavement with a couple of beat-up mitts and an old tennis ball.

One slow summer day in August, Billy and Big Joe decided to play a game of marbles after a practice session with the Wildcats. The alleys and side streets that were adjacent to Sixth Avenue were not paved. They were dirt streets and alleys in dry weather and muddy messes on rainy days.

Marbles was a fun game in those days, and the dirt side streets made a perfect arena on which to play. The game was played by each player placing a determined number of marbles in the center of a ring about six feet in diameter. Each player in turn "knuckles down" on the circumference of the circle and, with his favorite "shooter marble," tries to knock the center ones out of the ring and claim them as his own. The game engendered a language all its own with favorite marbles identified as Glassies or Aggies or Bull's-eyes. A great triumph in a game of marbles would be to knock an opponent's shooter out of the ring if it failed to exit the circle without itself hitting a center marble out. It was a quiet distraction from the boys' usual preoccupation with baseball. Moms also liked the idea that the boys were in sight at the corner and not down at the ball field for endless hours doing "God knows what!"

While Billy and Big Joe were drawing their circle in the dirt preparing for their game, Billy noticed that Jayroy was watching from his front steps about a half block away. Billy realized that Jayroy was new at the public school and called out an invitation to join the game. Jayroy walked over, and in a short time, they awkwardly exchanged information about themselves. Jayroy declined the offer to play, saying that he didn't have any marbles, and as Billy was about to offer him a loan of some of his, a crack of a .22 rifle split the air as a bullet whined above the three boys grazing a telephone pole next to their marble circle.

The wall of the dead end street protected the residents from an abandoned stone quarry which served as a refuge for the homeless, a verdant 'jungle' for adventurous boys, and also as convenient garbage dump prior to more sanitary waste disposal methods.

On this corner, the boys played a game of marbles when a .22 bullet grazed the pole above their heads.

The sound of a .22 rifle was not in itself unusual on a dead-end street overlooking a dumping site. Men, young and old, would often stand on the stone wall and shoot at rats that were foraging in the garbage below. The intended targets at the dump site were 180 degrees in the opposite direction from where the boys were playing marbles, and it was very unlikely for a bullet to take that path. It would also be impossible to suggest that there might have been a stray ricochet off a rock or piece of metal, since anyone with right intent to kill rats would be aiming down into the quarry where aimless bullets would be swallowed by the cavernous rocks below.

The boys were startled. They knew what the whining sound was, and they saw the splintered side of the pole that took the force of the bullet. Jayroy was especially concerned. He heard his parents talk about their movement to "this part of town." It seems they had no choice, for whatever reason Jayroy did not know, but the move was supposed to be temporary until they would rejoin other family members in the friendlier confines of the lower riverside streets where "people of our kind" lived. Jayroy went home quickly, and Billy and Gussie picked up their marbles and walked toward their homes, wondering whether or not they should tell their parents what had happened.

Billy had a special relationship with his mom. She had a mom's radar that picked up concern on his face or detected any change in his mannerisms that said something "is wrong, but I don't know if I should tell you."

"What's wrong, Billy? You look troubled," she said, before he could even put his marble bag away.

Billy began to protest the typical teen protest that nothing was wrong and maybe she should stop picking on him, when his mother's face betrayed a slight grin that told him it was useless to try to fool her with any more fake teen bravado. He told her about the bullet shot above their heads soon after Jayroy had joined them at the marble ring. They both thought the same unthinkable thought that the rifle shot may have been a warning. She sighed a sigh that reflected her own previous concerns over how some of the neighbors might react when the Smith family moved into the neighborhood. She tried to assure Billy that, basically, the folks on the block were decent people, but "there are always a few bad eggs in the crate." She did not quite convince herself, and Billy, with a bit of kid's radar of his own, picked up on the veiled anguish in his mother's voice. They talked for a long time about the racial issues of black and white. She was a woman ahead of her times in many ways.

They decided that what they could do now was show a bit of kindness to the Smith family, hope that the incident really was an accidental occurrence of a stray bullet, and finally, that nothing of this would be mentioned to Billy's dad, whose explosive disposition might prompt him to take his shotgun down to the quarry in search of some different kind of "rats." It was not the first time that

Billy and his mom conspired to withhold information from his dad. "What one doesn't know can't hurt you," was mom's rationalization. And in this case, she may have been right.

The two talked at great length about the co-mingling lives of the races. She revealed to her son that as a young girl, she witnessed a burning cross high on the hillside across the river from the very town in which they now lived. She told Billy of the clandestine Ku Klux Klan and their fiery symbol of racial superiority. She was told as a youngster, that it was not only a warning to Negroes but to Catholics and Jews as well. Catholics were thought to be heretical Christians planning to follow their anti-Christ pope to the Whitehouse and take over the country; Jews, on the other hand, were out to dominate the entire world with their subversive power in the banking and entertainment industries. The KKK's discontent with Negroes was expressed by the fear of contaminating the white race through inter-marriage with a subhuman species.

Billy listened in silence as his mother quietly spoke of the unfairness of this racial prejudice. Billy went to public school with both black and Jewish students. He never connected the social dots as to why the black kids lived in a different part of town and the Jewish kids did not seem to understand the Lord's Prayer that was recited by the class in homeroom every day. His sandlot baseball team was made up of mostly ethnic Italian American kids who all went to the same Catholic church, and he never questioned the homogeneous makeup of the team. They were all his friends. He was pretty friendly with the other kids in his class as well, including the Jewish and black kids. He was confused when he learned of the plight of the blacks under the Jim Crow laws of the South.

Billy's cousin—his mother's nephew—had been a captain in the Marine Corps during the Second World War. He was proud of his cousin, Frank, who commanded an all-black Marine brigade and always spoke highly of the bravery of his men under the horrific fighting in the South Pacific. Billy never understood anything about segregation of the races—especially in the military. He was getting a powerful and painful lesson in social justice and the lack of it. The very Marines that fought for their country on the bloody beaches of

Iwo Jima were denied housing in the north and relegated to separate drinking fountains in the south. Such was Billy's education regarding justice in America, and he began processing all the information he garnered since experiencing that momentous day with Jayroy under the telephone pole and his mother's quiet and secretive talk.

About two weeks after the marble incident, Billy saw from his living room window that Jayroy was outside of his house playing catch again with William. Billy was surprised to see Reds cross the street from his house three doors from Billy and engage Jayroy in a conversation. Only the back of Reds was visible to Billy, but he could see Jayroy smiling slightly and nodding his head in an agreement with whatever Reds was saying.

Reds had invited Jayroy to play with the Sixth Avenue Wildcats. Apparently, Reds had his leadership eye on Jayroy long before Billy or any of the boys even considered including an outsider who was new to the tight-knit neighborhood in any of their activities. Billy had never imagined that his invitation to play marbles on their street corner would be extended to joining their precious ball team. Apart from watching Jayroy throw the ball around with his little brother, Billy had no idea of Jayroy's baseball talent or lack thereof. Reds, as usual, knew differently. How, no one was sure. Jayroy was a very good player. Reds knew he could pitch, and when not pitching, he played anywhere in the infield. His favorite position was second base, and it was years later that an adult Billy found out why. It seems that the Brooklyn Dodgers had signed a player out of the Negro League to their minor league franchise in Montreal. Jackie Robinson was the player's name, and Jayroy knew all about this remarkable player who starred in many sports at UCLA and was now playing in an all-black baseball league.

Jayroy played with the Wildcats that summer in about six games. He pitched against the Spring Mill Blue Jays in one game in which Big Joe drove in three runs in a 4–2 victory. Ernie said that catching Jayroy was like "sitting in a rocking chair," and that "he hit my glove wherever I set it out." Ernie's enthusiasm expressed the very same quote that he read from the Phillies catcher at that time, Andy

Seminick, but Ernie himself was a much better catcher than an original phrase-maker.

Regardless, Jayroy was accepted pretty much by the Wildcats and by most of the opposing teams. There was one incident against a faraway team from North Wales that Reds had booked as a "non-league" game. It was a close game when Jayroy led off the bottom of the fifth with a sharp single to left. On the very next pitch with Gussie up at the plate, Jayroy took off from first and stole second. He promptly stole third on the second pitch and so unnerved the pitcher that he proceeded to walk the next two batters, loading the bases. Big Joe promptly cleared the bases with a might double, breaking up the game, which eventually turned into a "laugher." There is no question that Jayroy was the spark that turned that game around. The team they beat that day was not one of their usual neighborhood rivals, and at the end of the game, Reds was seen talking rather seriously but calmly to one of the leaders of the opposing team. It seems that a remark was made in reference to Jayroy as they were leaving the field, and Reds wanted some clarification. When all of the Sixth Avenue boys saw this uneasy encounter they went immediately to where Reds was talking to several of the other team members. Reds assured his teammates that everything was cool, and the teams dispersed to their separate destinations. Reds never booked a game with them again and would only say that they did not like being "shown up" by a "colored boy." Reds told the boys out of earshot of Jayroy who was already on his way home. He never participated in the after-game ritual of gulping down milkshakes at Jessie's soda fountain.

Reds had handled the situation by suggesting to the unhappy visitors that they should get a better catcher who might be able to throw runners out. Reds doubted that they would be playing that team again.

It would be much later that an adult Billy as a high school social science teacher would piece together the racial prejudice that seemed to slowly emerge along with the transition from childhood through adolescence and into adulthood. There seem to be a direct proportionate relationship: the more one became an adult, the more one became biased. It was as if children were poured out of a vast ocean of innocence and funneled into a narrow stream of bias and bigotry. The Rodgers and Hammerstein musical of 1949, in which a young navy lieutenant falls in love with a girl from the South Pacific Islands reflects how the innocence of childhood is shaped by the socially constructed prejudices perpetrated by the privileged majority. Realizing that his family back in Philadelphia will never accept her as one of the family, he sings the sorrowful song, "You have to be carefully taught." We are all born as open books without bias, until we are taught—to hate and fear the other, those who are unlike us.

Billy was the only boy from the Sixth Avenue gang to go on to college. He was inspired in many ways by his civics teacher whose enthusiasm and love of his discipline stuck to Billy like Velcro. Also, Billy did not need much prodding to study. He actually loved school. His mom had taught him how to read before he enrolled in formal schooling. Every Friday evening, his mother took him for the short walk into the town's shopping district. At the corner 5 & 10 Woolworth Store, Billy was allowed to choose a Big Little Book. This was a popular series of adventure books for kids, given their unlikely name by their odd design. The books were almost square in shape, about four inches by four and a half inches, but with the thickness of over four hundred pages. They were *Big Little Books*. For ten cents, a kid could get lost in the adventures of Dick Tracey or travel to the moon with Buck Rogers. Billy had an insatiable appetite for reading, and these adventure books occupied much of his time— too much perhaps when they interfered with his chores expected of him by his father.

Maybe the educational opening to a larger world through the unlikely door of Big Little Books marked Billy for a teaching career, but there he was teaching youngsters about subject matters he himself never learned in school such as social justice and the injustice of Jim Crow. The experience with Jayroy that summer changed Billy in many ways. Jayroy played only one summer with the Sixth Avenue Wildcats. That fall, his family moved to the other side of town on the street next to the river where the other African American families lived. Maybe it was that .22 rifle shot that provoked the move; maybe the family needed the comfort of being "with their own kind."

Whatever the case, it was a loss for the Sixth Avenue team, but more importantly, a loss for any concept of American ideals of equality and social justice. Billy apparently never forgot that summer with Jayroy. They still met of course at school and on the high school baseball team, or at the ticket window of the local movie house before Jayroy went in to sit in the unspoken section for "his kind." In many ways, they lived separate social lives. Apart from official school sports activities and classroom meetings, they never really interacted. The school had a terrific dance band, a twenty-piece orchestra with a big band sound that would do Glenn Miller proud. The band played at all the school dances and some of the talented members were black kids who lived in that lower part of town. Regardless of the band members, no other blacks attended the dance as a social or recreational activity. They just did not. They all lived in the same small town, went to the same school, played on the same sport's team, frequented the same movie theater, and yet were separated by an invisible social barrier that prohibited the full interactive association of civil life.

The full impact of this inequity struck Billy when, as an adult, he learned of the Negro Baseball League that had a storied history of outstanding ball players that ran a parallel and separate course of history alongside of the baseball feats that Billy knew and loved so well.

This revelation that there existed in America a professional baseball league of "colored" players was something that mystified Billy. Not only that there existed such a league but in the very same city of Philadelphia where the boys would see the American League Athletics and the National League Phillies play, there was a team in the Negro League called the Philadelphia Stars. How could the boys not know? How could a free and open society as the American democracy manage to keep such a monumental fact of America's pastime concealed from the majority population? Billy was especially dumfounded and confused over this revelation. How, in a free and open society like America, could he *not* know of the League and the Philadelphia Stars, and how they played at Passon Field in West Philadelphia? Sometimes, they even played at Shibe Park, that mecca of green delight in the middle of the city where the boys' worshipped the feats of the lowly Philadelphia Athletics and Phillies. Shibe Park, where Billy's father took him to see his first night game. He remembered what a feeling of awe, when he went from the dark city streets of North Philadelphia, through the narrow tunnel that opened up on a bright spectacular lighted field.

Billy, as an adult teacher of the young, often reflected on that first night game at Shibe Park where an invisible team played, only when the A's and the Phillies were absent. Unbelievable? But of course, many people other than the blacks who attended their game *did* know. They must have known, even though the news of anything black never travelled beyond the pages of the black newspapers that were as isolated and segregated as the very people for whom they wrote. Just as Billy and his friends and the majority of white people knew where the blacks lived and where they sat in the theatre, and where they picnicked together on holidays in a remote grassy part of town. People saw without seeing, they heard without hearing, they cared without caring. The paradox of knowing and not knowing is prompted by the human feeling of "care." The more one cares about anything, the more significant is their knowledge; the less care, the less significant the knowledge. In this way, the majority of people could take a wide path around, or avoid entirely, the place where blacks had their picnics or sit as far away as possible from the all-black section in the movies. They knew the blacks were there, but did not care to engage them. They moved on parallel tracks that never met.

The all-American game of baseball, the nation's pastime, reflected this parallel world of blacks and whites that existed in the community. The microcosmic dualism of baseball mirrored the macrocosmic community of two worlds.

Billy's shame at never bringing such an obvious fact to the forefront of his knowledge engendered a sense of guilt in him. He resolved as a teacher to open the minds of his students in his history and social science classes. He convinced the administrators where he taught to incorporate a new approach to social sciences called "multiculturalism." The texts would include the contributions of diverse groups that had previously been written out of the history of America. Billy reflected on his own history courses when he was in high school. The history he learned was much sanitized to say the least. America was the land of freedom and opportunity and the poor persecuted pilgrims set the trends of tolerance and goodness in the New World of endless opportunities. The settlers made friends with the "Indians;" Pocahontas was a princess who married an Englishman and became a Christian. The Civil War was over—in three pages—the North won, the slaves freed, and everyone lived happily ever after. There evidently could not be a hint of any controversial historical event in America.

Billy knew that all this glossing of history was well intentioned and not meant to slight any group from recognition of their true contributions to American society. He also knew that by this "benign" ignoring many deeds of people, especially those of minority populations, allowed a breeding ground of negative stereotyping by the very omission of the positive roles they played in society.

In the early 1960s, Billy introduced his class to John Howard Griffin's book, *Black Like Me*. It is an extraordinary story of the author's six-week trip through the Deep South as a black man. Griffin chemically darkened the color of his skin and shaved his head and passed as black in a South that he had previously known as a white man. All the politeness, cordiality. and genteelness of the white man's South turned into a vile cauldron of hatred and degradation. This highly educated white man could get no job other than cleaning the public lavatories at a train station. He heeded the prohibition of making direct eye contact with any passing whites. He experienced the humiliation of dancing when asked by a passing white man who needed confirmation that the "coloreds" are really happy-go-lucky people.

Perhaps the most poignant experience of Griffin's book occurred when he stopped to rest at a sharecropper's shack where he was given food and drink. The family's small children were playing happily around the kitchen table. Griffin remarked to the father that his children seemed so happy. The tired sharecropper replied, "Don't you know why? They don't know yet that they are black."

Chapter Four

Billy's Notebook Part I: Witness to a Hero

*B*illy was the only "Wildcat" to go on to college after high school. *He eventually became a teacher. Here is an unedited paper written by Billy which, quite possibly, has never been seen by any one until now. Billy, it seemed, was preparing to write a series of articles for a local newspaper. He planned to call the series "Billy's Notebook."*

Billy had never bragged about the time his father took him to a night game at old Shibe Park in 1947 when Jackie Robinson made his debut in Philadelphia playing for the Brooklyn Dodgers. It is not known if the other boys knew about this trip. It would be strange if they did not, but the boys never talked much about what they did with their parents, and since Billy's father was accompanied by the father's peers—well, their behavior might have been an embarrassment for Billy. Here is one of his articles—"Witness to a Hero."

Mythology tells of heroes undertaking enormous feats of endurance and trial in search of something that will benefit humankind. The hero on a quest is a universal metaphor for human accomplishments performed under great duress. We human beings need our heroes. We are born with the burden of our own fragility and mortality. We need hope and inspiration in the face of both known and unknown perils of life. We gain vicarious strength through the deeds

34

of heroes. Heroes are born in dark times of civilization's needs. They face great adversity, threats on their lives, mortal enemies, evil personified. The hero quest becomes a morality play writ large— with the hero lighting the way of goodness and casting evil in bold relief. Some have claimed that our modern age has witnessed the death of the heroic figure. Is it true? If so, who has wielded the death blow to the hero? Economic greed? Technology? Relativity? Post-Modernism? Cynicism? Is the hero really dead? Paul Simon's musical score for the 1967 film *The Graduate* laments the demise of the hero and asks, "Where have you gone, Joe DiMaggio, our lonely nation turns her eyes to you?" It is curious that a professional baseball player was heralded as the last American hero. Was Joe DiMaggio a hero? Perhaps. Certainly he embodied the mythic proportions of the game he played. Baseball was America's pastime. The game represented everything good about this young country—fair play, sportsmanship, ingenuity, versatile skills, team spirit, unity of purpose. Any youngster in America who could dream, could find his field of dreams on a baseball diamond. The game was a metaphor for life. You could make it in America. You could be Joe DiMaggio. But you had to be white.

On April 15, 1947, Jackie Robinson became the first African American to play professional baseball in the major leagues. He played for the Brooklyn Dodgers. That is correct, the BROOKLYN Dodgers, and any other claim to that team name is made by a pretender —at least to anyone familiar with that era of Jackie Robinson, Pee Wee Reese, Gil Hodges, Duke Snyder, et al. They were the Brooklyn Dodgers and were a team destined for social history when Jackie Robinson took his position at Ebbets Field on April 15, 1947. The nation-wide attention was stunning—and so was the racial animosity. The black-white chasm that already existed in this country (fourteen years before civil rights legislation) was widened further by Robinson's entry into major league ball. Never mind that Robinson was an exemplary human being—gifted both intellectually and athletically. At UCLA, Robinson excelled not only in baseball, but in track, football and basketball. He would have truly qualified for the sometimes-loose–fitting cognomen of today, "student athlete." The abuses that Robinson suffered from both players and the public are well documented. He was grist for the public and private mills of prejudice.

The testimony that this writer offers is of the personal type. I saw Jackie Robinson play in 1947. My father frequently took me to Shibe Park at Twenty-First and Lehigh Avenue in North Philadelphia. It was home field for the Philadelphia Phillies and the Philadelphia Athletics (there is *another* pretender in Oakland). Usually we went to see the A's play —they had a more glorious history than the Phils. This evening, however, we were going to see the Phillies play the Dodgers and see what this Jackie Robinson was all about. I was only a teenager at this time, but remember the evening very well when I joined my father and his buddies (they would be called a "posse" today) to see the ominous Dodgers—made more forbidding with Robinson—take on the hapless Phillies.

I remember clearly that the entire ballpark was preoccupied with Robinson. The sound from the stands resonated in response to his actions when he batted, when he ran the bases, when he had fielding opportunities. I remember the cruel epithets hurled at him from the people around me. I remember my father's guilty side-glances in my direction after he joined his gang in voicing some racial opinions of his own. I also remember his acknowledgment that we had watched a very talented player that night. He confessed this to me at a safe distance from his friends. Even at a tender teen age I had seen and played enough baseball to know that Jackie Robinson was indeed a talented player (he won the batting title in 1949 with a .342 average). I also knew he was the same color as several families that lived across from my row house in a small town, six blocks from the Schuylkill River. My schoolmates and teammates lived in those homes. I lived on an integrated street and to me as a youngster, an integrated base-ball team did not seem to be a big deal.

I did not know much about mythic heroes then either. I was still a few years away from high school Latin class when we studied Virgil's *Aeneid*. My personal assessment of Robinson's heroism is ret-rospective. He faced personal peril for the sake of a common good. He assumed the opprobrium of a hateful people that exposed the vileness of that hatred to public view. He surrendered his human propensity to retaliate against his tormentors so that the evil of racism would stand exposed for what it is—ugly. Few people can claim the moral courage to do what he did. Few people have the opportunity or the strength to face what he faced. He was, indeed, a hero and sixty-three years ago on a warm night in North Philadelphia I was witness to his heroism.

Billy saw Robinson play against the Phillies in 1947

Chapter Five

"The Phillies Are Coming"

Reds broke the news one summer morning when the Wildcats were gathering for a game against the Ninth Avenue Pirates. Reds, in his infinite quest for fairness and impartiality, wanted the Pirates to know as well that the Phillies were holding an open-tryout session at the Elmwood Park field in Norristown—one town over from where the boys lived. The tryout would be a week from Saturday, and rides would be coordinated—most of the boys were over sixteen now and already experienced drivers. Some might ask their parents to drive them to the park—if they promised not to embarrass the boys.

This was big news! "Who would believe the Phillies would send professional scouts to 'our neck of the woods'?" Big Joe exclaimed.

"They're gonna pick you, Reds, they're gonna pick you," stammered Gussie. "Wait till they see how you can play shortstop *and* pitch. Oh yeah, wait till they see Big Joe smash the ball."

This was Ernie: "They're gonna sign him up on the spot!"

"Don't forget Billy's speed," said Reds, who reminded the boys of Billy's skills in running down fly balls.

The enthusiasm generated by the news that the Phillies were coming spilled over into the game on this particular day and the boys—both sides—never played better. Every hit, every catch, every stolen base was executed with additional flair and perfection as the boys wish-fulfilled their play before the eyes of the highly anticipated

Phillies scouts. It was, as it were, a perfect dress rehearsal for "the Bigs." Reds was magnificent—pitching the first five innings and playing a flawless shortstop the last four. Big Joe hit two home runs; Billy was three for four with two stolen bases and two runs scored; Gussie, perhaps the least-skilled player, snared a sinking line drive in right and doubled the runner off second base. And in a record-breaking at bat, Ernie reached second base with a double, breaking his longest singles record. Even his pants stayed up.

The stopover at Jesse's soda fountain after the game was exceptionally exuberant. They jabbered about their elevated level of play and talked about Saturday and their big "tryout" with the Phillies. Now it must be admitted that the honesty and openness of youth also brings with it a certain naiveté. Other patrons of Jesse's soda fountain were already past the threshold of adulthood and unloaded their more-mature cynicism in the direction of the boys. "The Phillies aren't coming to see you guys play," they mocked. The boys were undaunted in their enthusiasm for Saturday's big day, although it must be admitted that they grew silent. They often practiced this turtle-like defense mechanism of pulling back when confronted with grown-up "downers." A keen observer would not fail to notice, however, that while they did not retaliate against their older tormentors, they did exchange smiling glances from their lowered heads, signaling to each other that nothing had dimmed their joyful expectations about Saturday.

So on a bright and sunny Saturday, the Wildcats found their way to Elmwood Park—along with over a thousand other boys. The first clue the boys should have gotten that these "tryouts" may not be what they anticipated was when the scouts came on to the field after alighting from some badly dented and rundown vans. They did not exactly arrive by first-class transportation. In addition, instead of the men they imagined to be attired in sparkling Phillies uniforms, these guys were pretty seedy looking—in baggy nondescript sweatshirts and shapeless trousers, which may or may not have been belted below their paunches. They did have baseball spikes on—the boys conceded that to their baseball expertise.

The second disappointing clue was the number of youngsters that showed up at the park. It resembled a call for extras at a Cecil B. DeMille extravaganza film shoot. All kids of every size and shape were there, pushing and shoving to get closer to the "scouts" who seemed too preoccupied with their clip boards to pay attention to them. After what felt like an eternity of time, the mob of boys was organized by positions. The plan was to rotate players at each position every time three batters were thrown five pitches each. The net result was a constant rush of players on and off the field while a long line of hitters pushed and shoved to be closer to the plate for their turn at bat. While one of the man-scouts was doing the pitching, another scout was hitting fly balls with a fungo bat to a horde of kids jostling for position in the overly crowded outfield. A third jowly scout was hitting ground balls to rotating infielders who sometimes had to choose between fielding the grounders hit by the coach or the ones hit by the batters. One poor kid near the third base bag hesitated too long and "caught" two balls at the same time—one with his face and the other with his stomach. It wasn't pretty. Let it be noted that he was not one of the Wildcats.

Unfortunately, our Wildcats did not fare much better. Maybe they were overwhelmed by the moment. Reds was lucky enough to be selected in the first group of batters and patiently waited his turn to hit. As soon as he stepped in the box, the scout who had been pitching decided to turn over his role to those kids who fancied themselves as future pitchers. The very first pitch to Reds came directly at his head—hard! Reds unceremoniously dropped his bat and hit the dirt. The scouts all laughed—and maybe it was funny, but the kids should have been given the opportunity to laugh first and they did not. It just wasn't the same as playing their own game at their own park. To make things worse, Reds swung and missed three times. Reds never struck out. He went on to be one of the best athletes at the local high school, and yet here under these strained and artificial conditions, he looked terrible. They all did. Billy, a terrific centerfielder, dropped a routine fly ball that he normally would put in his back pocket. Poor Ernie never got a chance to catch and show off his great arm and never got a turn at bat. He seemed to be a step too slow for the quickly timed rotations.

One would think that the dismal experience would have really put the boys in a major funk. But one should never underestimate the resiliency of the young and the amazing plasticity of their psyche. The boys came home with an indomitable swagger that merited extra-large black-and-white milkshakes at Jesse's. You would think they had been signed to a Phillies farm team.

All in all, their original joy over the Phillies tryouts was not pure naiveté. It wasn't the first time nor the last that major league clubs would send local scouts to their area. Just a few years after our boys had a less-than-successful tryout, the Brooklyn Dodgers sent some serious scouts to watch a skinny young left-handed pitcher from Norristown who was playing American Legion Ball on that same field where our boys had their own tryouts. It was not long after their visit that the Dodgers signed Tommy Lasorda to their club as a highly touted prospect to become a big league star. Of course, Lasorda did become a baseball success, but not in the brief three-year career as a pitcher. His well-known fame came as a manager and a baseball executive for the Brooklyn/Los Angeles Dodgers. Stories such as these vindicated the enthusiasm that the boys had over this privileged opportunity to play before major league scouts—no matter how lowly the scouts were or how poorly the boys played. It was still fun.

Chapter Six

Saturday Afternoon Matinée

T he boys' hometown had two movie theaters: the old and decrepit Forest Theater was a rundown burlesque house that had long seen its day. It was on a remote side street on the lower part of town and could be reached only by those who knew what they were looking for. The colorless seats were old and faded and most of them broken or split with stuffing hanging out and battered arm rests. Its interior was dark and drab with no renovated touches in years. It had a pungent odor that suggested to olfactory powers that something had died in there—animal or vegetable one could not say. One's shoes stuck to floor as a warning that therein may be the source of the former life that now emits the foul aroma. The movies shown at the unfortunate Forest Theater, which only opened on weekends, were reruns of old cowboy movies featuring Gene Autry or Hopalong Cassidy.

In contrast, the Riant was a newer movie house located on the brightly lit main street of town in the heart of the three-block business section. The Riant carried the deserved reputation of being a first-class theater for its time, with ornate gold-leaf trim, vaulted ceiling, and enormous side murals depicting scenes from the Greek muses of art. Originally built also as a stage theatre, the Riant was renovated for motion pictures and was rightly proud of showing "first-run movies," meaning, that the humbler folks in small-town

USA saw the same released films that the fancy city slickers saw in Philadelphia.

The distinction between city life and suburban life was different in the era of the Sixth Avenue Wildcats. There were no suburbs then as we now know them. The gentrification of the suburbs was a long way off. There were small towns along the river where blue-collar families struggled in low-paying jobs at dangerous mills that produced steel and boilers and batteries and car tires. Billy's uncle worked in the boiler plant and was struck in the head by a boiler that swung loose from the assembly line. He survived on a meager disability pension provided by the disinterested boiler factory. Reds's neighbor returned from World War II to his young wife and two small children and was burned to death in a gas explosion at the steel plant. Life in the big city, on the other hand, ignored the pockets of poverty and reveled in the power that their fine educational institutions offered. The art museums, the concert halls, the symphony orchestra, the universities—all were markers of municipal success.

Thus did the Riant theater offer the one parallel experience with the big city. The folks of small town saw the same movies at the same time as their big city neighbors. And they were proud of that.

The Riant theater had a balcony, which was occasionally frequented by Reds and his buddies—at least once a month, more often if a good serial accompanied the feature attraction. Then it would be every week to see how Batman and Robin survived the precarious peril of facing instant death, which seemed imminent at the end of each episode. Buster Crabbe's portrayal of Buck Rogers was another good serial grabber that would ensure weekly returns by the boys.

It was the main feature attraction, however, that would be the ultimate reason for going to the movies on Saturday afternoon. A new Tarzan movie was always a sure winner in getting the boys to the movies. Tarzan was played by the incomparable Johnny Weissmuller, who had parlayed Olympic fame as a swimmer into a very successful Hollywood career. Tall, handsome, Weissmuller, with that gravelly voice and Tarzan yell that could never be duplicated by later pretenders to the role. And Jane and Cheetah in supporting roles were favorites of the fans. Jane, played by Maureen O'Sullivan, was every boy's dream. The epitome of female innocence and beauty, dressed in skimpy skins of animal hide, awakened in many boys the latent desire for the opposite sex. The boys were still a little way off from discovering girls, but "Jane" would serve as a subconscious model for all that was good and pure about womanhood. And that wasn't bad.

What was true of substituting a new Tarzan for Weissmuller was also true of putting in a new Jane. It was totally unacceptable. Maybe the boys drifted away from Tarzan movies in the natural process of growing up and might have nothing to do with their rejection of different actors in the respective roles. On the other hand, there might be a legitimate factor of identifying with any art form and rejecting any attempt to change it. Well into maturity, people will reject different renditions of their favorite songs, disdain remakes of their favorite old-time movies, shrug off all attempts that try to duplicate the original artistic version of the good old days. Whatever happened to the "Big Band" sound of Glenn Miller and Tommy Dorsey and Benny Goodman? What's the matter with kids today!

The *Dead End Kids* was another feature presentation favorite of the gang. Leo Gorcey played the leader of the gang as "Mugsy," a hard-bitten scrapper with his crown hat on the back of his head and wise cracks coming out of the side of his mouth as eternal nuggets of wisdom. One of Mugsy's sidekicks was "Satch" played by Huntz Hall. Satch was the loyal but dumb counterweight to Mugsy—the straight man to Mugsy's quips.

The *Dead End Kids* was originally a Broadway play by Sidney Kingsley depicting the harsh life of a group of kids growing up in the slums of New York City. Reds and his buddies saw the very end of the era of the *Dead End Kids*, when all their mean vandal-tough behavior was sanitized into light, comical movies that conveyed a clear moral message. Mugsy and his gang wind up rescuing helpless small-store owners from unscrupulous loan sharks or saving a young and vulnerable widow from the clutches of a venomous tenement landlord. Shortly after the Wildcats out grew the *Dead End Kids*, they became the Bowery Boys, which gave even more respectability—and perhaps a more innocuous shift to their ever-changing shapes.

The irony that these dead-ender film stars appealed to Reds and his buddies reside in the fact that the Wildcats actually lived on a dead-end street in their own small town. There had been a stone quarry at the edge of town from which many crude stones were lovingly hewn into aesthetic materials used in some of the most beautiful churches and mansions of the town. The owners of the factories, mills, and plants lived in those mansions; the Irish, Polish, and Italian immigrants prayed in the churches. The Italian stone masons were the craftsmen who contributed the stone to these structures. Reds's grandfather worked in that stone quarry and lost an arm in a dynamite explosion. The company semiretired him as a one-armed security guard. Legend has it that Reds's grandfather could handle a shot gun with one arm better than anyone with *due bracci*. The quarry was closed long before the boys were born, and the street sealed off fittingly by a four-foot stone wall preventing a precipitous drop to the bottom. The only remnants of the quarry were the huge sides of sheer stone that formed the quarry and the markings etched in those walls where the last stone had been taken. There was also a rusted steel cable trapped permanently in the earth not far from the dead-end wall. Adventurous boys called this "The Monkey Slide" and would shimmy to the bottom by hanging from the cable with hands attached in front and their legs wrapped around the bottom. They would slowly descend monkey-like to the bottom of the quarry, which was overgrown with trees and plants and wild bushes. Many a slide down to the quarry bottom would be accompanied by facsimile Tarzan yells, which were perfectly consistent with the quarries overgrown vegetation. Alas, these young Tarzans did not have any Janes.

The boys also enjoyed going to Abbott and Costello movies. These two comedians from nearby New Jersey were national favorites. Short on plot and story line but long on laughter and zaniness, Bud Abbott and Lou Costello never failed to fill the movie house with packed audiences. Straight man Abbott and comic Costello appealed to the budding sense of wit and irony developing in the young audience.

Every birthday, Billy's godmother took him on the train to Philadelphia for a dinner and a show. This was the ultimate trifecta for a small-town kid. A train ride in and of itself was no mean feat. It was expensive, relatively speaking, to ride the train; and Philadelphia seemed so far away and so culturally different to a small-towner that the trip itself needed months to plan. Secondly, going out to a restaurant was unheard of for first-generation Americans. Money was hard to come by, and it seemed like such a waste to pay someone else other than mom or grandmom to cook the food! Eating at a restaurant for no other reason than enjoyment seemed almost like a matter for confession. One can almost hear the immigrant priest say incredulously from behind the screened confessional, "You did what? Eat at a restaurant?" One who knew how hard the people worked for their money and how little they got paid for their labors can understand the guilt that might accompany such a frivolous outing. Yet his godmother—aunt, thought so much of Billy that they made this expedition to the big city once a year. And not only to ride a train and eat at a restaurant, but also, to see a live stage show at the Earle Theater in the heart of downtown Philadelphia. And what do you suppose Billy and his aunt saw live on stage at the Philly theater this particular year? Bud Abbott and Lou Costello performing their signature act, "Who's on First." It was a rare privilege to see live this marvelously funny routine, demanding exquisite timing of the double-meaning names of Abbott's baseball team. Billy never failed to remind his envious buddies whenever they saw Abbott and Costello in the movies. He would have bragged even more had he known then that this classic skit would claim a place in the Baseball Hall of Fame in Cooperstown.

Juji fruits were the favorite candy of the balcony sitters. These hard-jellied, fruit-flavored tooth-rotters had all kinds of side benefits. Besides affording a long-lasting treat in the mouth (they were long in dissolving and penalized the hurried taster who bit into it by sticking tenaciously to one's teeth), Juji fruits also served as convenient missiles that could be projected onto the people seated in the orchestra. This latter use of Jujis ran the risk of an usher's flashlight warning, that was at once a fear and a tempting challenge. How far can one go in advancing the cause of chicanery—like throwing a Juji fruit— without risking the usher's putting the flashlight of shame on you and possibly expelling you from the theater? Let it be known that no Wildcat was ever ejected from the Riant theater although they experienced vicarious fear and shame with the removal of many a kid on any given Saturday matinee.

The Riant theatre, where the boys of Sixth Avenue saw many matinees. Abbott and Costello films were among their favorites. Courtesy of Jack & Brian Coll

Chapter Seven

Sunday School . . . and Wednesday School

T he boys of the Sixth Avenue Wildcats were mostly sons of Italian immigrants—most of the boys were first generation Americans. Billy, for example, was three years old when his father became a naturalized citizen changing his name—with great pride, from Antonio to Anthony. Since they were several generations by birth behind their Irish brethren of the same Catholic faith, they were significantly behind in economic security. The beautiful stone Irish Catholic Church stood proudly next to an equally beautiful school where the sons and daughters of the O'Briens and Callahans and Murphys worshiped and studied respectively. The Italian villagers prayed in a basement church and had no sufficient funds to raise stones to the heavens or even build a parochial school. Not being members of the Irish parish, these children attended the local public school, along with their Polish-American neighbors, who also had no school of their own. Overall, the public school housed a wide variety of every ethnic and religious group possible. It was truly a multicultural experience simply to attend this small and intimate school—before multiculturalism or diversity or pluralism was ever considered to be a worthy subject of study.

And so it happened that the Catholic kids who attended the public school received no formal training in their religion at school.

Their Irish counterparts had religious instructions built into the school curriculum. Every Sunday, therefore, after the nine o'clock children's mass, all the Italian "public" kids were required to stay in the church and receive religious instructions. Two sisters of a religious order would walk the four blocks or so to the Italian church, organize the kids into the pews for Mass, admonish them for any bad behavior, and give then cues for kneeling, standing, and sitting with a click of a tin cricket hidden in the folds of their sleeves.

The travels of the good sisters every Sunday from the Irish convent across town to save the little public school heathens from the clutches of Satan had all the earmarks of a missionary tale. Girls, considered obsequious by the boys, would wait as scouts spotting the two missionary sisters from two blocks away. Then they would run to the sisters and hand in hand accompany them to the church— much to the annoyance of the boys. Most Sunday school sessions involved learning the Baltimore Catechism by heart. There was an answer for any possible question of importance that a little boy or girl could have.

"Who made you?"

"God made me!"

"Why did God make you?"

"God made me to *know* Him, *love* Him, and *serve* Him in *this* world and be *happy* with Him in the *next!*" Asked and answered! The sing-song answers given in loud unison marked the children with an indelible seal of their faith—but also served as cover for those silent boys who had not memorized the answers.

Classes requiring special instructions in preparation for mega events, such as First Communion or Confirmation extended the Sunday school period. A lengthy Mass followed by a lengthier lesson in catechetic tested the endurance of the holy Wildcats as they frequently squirmed and shifted positions on the hard wooden pews of the church. Too much wiggling would prompt a threatening click from Sister St. Vincent's cricket. This warning had a similar effect as the movie usher's flashlight, except Sister Vincent would never expel the boys and they knew that. Being banished from the movies was a punishment; expulsion from Sunday school would have been a treat.

No, Sister Vincent would call a recalcitrant boy's parent if a sufficient number of warnings were not heeded. And no boy wanted that. A call to a parent telling them that their child was resisting the very Grace of God was a humiliating blow to the parent. To disgrace the child was to disgrace the parent, as if the rebuke came from an ambassador of God himself. No child wanted that, so it did not take too many clicks from Sister Vincent's cricket to have slouching backs straightened and wiggly bottoms stable on the polished wooden pews.

The Wildcats were all making their Confirmation this particular season. They were to become official soldiers of Christ. They were to be declared old enough to receive the sacramental grace that would strengthen them throughout their Catholic lives. True enough, Confession was always there to add a weekly or monthly vitamin boost of spirituality, and marriage would bring with it another booster shot of sacramental protection against new pitfalls that only married people might encounter; but it was confirmation that started you off on an adult Catholic life. The sacramental recipients must be prepared flawlessly for the special visit by the bishop. Extra time was needed for the select few, so other less-worthy kids were excused while the Confirmation kids remained to prepare for the holy event.

Part of the preparation involved learning a series of questions and answers that were appropriate for the occasion—questions that would relate to the sacrament and would be asked of the children by the bishop himself. Sister Vincent made it clear that there would be no disgraceful slip-ups. Every child was to know every answer to every question. Anyone embarrassing the parish, Sister Vincent, parents, and God Himself would suffer what might be worse than eternal damnation.

Now, the boys were paying more attention to how the good sister would have everyone seated in the pews in preparation for the big day. The children were separated—of course—boys on one side of the church aisle; girls on the other. There was no sense tempting the sacrament of strength beforehand. It was the order of the questions taught by Sister Vincent that drew their attention and so they concocted an ingenious plan to save them study time and satisfy sister, his excellency, and anyone else who might be offended by screwing up on such an important ritualistic day. The order of questions was already written up and the good sister never deviated from the pattern of asking the questions from right to left, from the aisle in toward the center. The questions were always asked in the same order; the boys were always seated in the same positions. End of discussion. Reds assigned one question to each boy so each had to learn one and only one answer to the question that would invariably be put to him and him alone.

In assigning the appropriate question-answer sequence in alignment with Reds's seating chart, he designated Billy as a wild card player. Reds would decide which question posed the longest and/ or hardest to answer and Billy would field that question. Reds knew that Billy could sit anywhere and answer any of the catechetical questions asked. He knew this from the many Sunday school preparatory sessions when sister would call on Billy to provide the correct answer for a faltering student fumbling miserably on the intricacies of redeeming graces. Billy was actually embarrassed for being asked to correct his school mates, but he had little choice. He simply had no problem in memorizing the answers. It wasn't his fault when one Sunday school day, Sister Vincent told him that his face was going to light up with radiance after he had corrected the fourth stumbling student in a row. Shoot, Billy knew that the only time his face lit up was when he nabbed that home run ball that Del Ennis had blasted into the left field upper deck. Now that was a miracle. None of Billy's teammates faulted him for this ignominious praise from sister. They knew Billy was kind of smart, but they accepted him for who he was—their teammate. Heck, they were glad he could be seated in position to take the toughest question and save them a lot of unnecessary brain power of memorizing words they that did not understand anyway.

Confirmation day came off without a hitch, with the boys in their Sunday best clothes, proud parents beaming with pride, sponsors as surrogate parents standing behind each boy. The bishop asked the questions and the boys gave the answers—flawlessly. Sister St. Vincent stood in the background hiding a few tiny tears of joy from her beloved rough and tumble angels. Each boy went up, received a slight tap on the cheek from his excellency to remind him of the expected obedience from Holy Mother the Church and received his new confirmation name and a small ring. The boys would admit that it was a special day, and their families made a big fuss over them with a Sunday dinner at home made to their specifications. Billy even got a new baseball mitt from his father—all for becoming a soldier of Christ.

The only reflective doubts they had came in their public school when they overheard Sidney Katzman telling some other kids about his Bar Mitzvah. The Catholic boys did not know anything about Judaism and were amazed at the comparable event occurring at the same age and representing a sort of rite of passage (although they would have never expressed it that way). No. What caught their attention was Sidney telling how he was the only kid honored that day and how proud he and his parents and the whole congregation in the synagogue were when he stood up alone and read from the Torah. He was an adult now, with the privilege of reading the sacred words for himself. The Wildcats thought briefly about how they had to share their Confirmation honors with about seventy-five other kids. Rather than reading the Good Book on their own, they recited from memory and were given a gentle but firm reminder from the bishop that unwavering obedience bled into adulthood. They did not dwell on these restrictive thoughts for long however, since the bell signaled physical education time and they all went tumbling down to the gym—Sidney included.

It was not only on Sunday after mass that the boys were taught their doctrinal lessons. The public school Catholic kids had to attend catechism classes on Wednesday afternoons as well. This came about when our boys were in the early stages of their high school careers. They were dismissed from the last period of school on Wednesdays if they had a note from their parents giving them permission to attend religious instructions at their church. Prior to this arrangement among parents and religious organizations was a curious practice. The public school in town, leavened by the well-intentioned Protestant fathers of early education in America, would have homeroom teachers—or designated students—read aloud to the class a short passage from the

King James Bible. This was the customary practice prior to lunch period in every homeroom. Following the reading the class would rise and recite the Lord's Prayer—more commonly known as the "Our Father." Now this presented a problem—in addition to the first amendment issue. Not all the students ended the prayer at the same time or the same verse. All the Catholics would end with "and lead us not into temptation, but deliver us from evil, Amen." The Protestant kids, however, kept on praying "for Thine is the Kingdom and the Power and the Glory forever and ever, Amen." Sid Katzman and the other Jewish kids were stumped from the very beginning of the prayer. They did not know what was going on. It was a lesson in multiculturalism strained beyond repair. Parents, especially the Catholic ones, began complaining about this time-honored tradition that had never been questioned before. Gussie's mom argued against using the King James Bible for the reading instead of the true Catholic version of God's word found in the Douay Bible. It may have been more a point of pride on the part of the moms rather than any serious doctrinal issues. Who knows? Although Billy's mom did argue that the Protestant version of the Christmas Gospel was incorrect when it offered, "Peace *and* Good Will to Men." She protested that the Douay version—the Catholic version—accurately stated, "Peace to Men *of* Good Will." Her own hermeneutics implying that one deserved God's peace only if you *had* Good Will. God knows how many rascals would stand in line—especially at Christmas, thinking they would get some "good will" they really did not deserve. "Well, maybe in the Protestant churches, but not in ours." She fulminated. This was the reasoning that supported the affront to the faith of Billy's mom. All things considered—not bad for one with only six formal years of schooling. Anyway, it was the protests of parents that led to the compromise policy of dismissing the students every Wednesday to the care of their respective churches. It was democracy in action.

Chapter Eight

...And Summer School

Public school kids needed extra-special religious training as an antidote against the heathen influence of being educated in a public school where one's immortal soul was placed in daily jeopardy of perdition. So in addition to the late-Wednesday afternoon sessions when the public sinners were released from school and sent to church for catechetical instructions, Reds and the gang were required to attend church summer school for the entire month of July—from nine until noon, Monday through Friday. Catholic school kids were evidently immunized against the evil temptations of summer in virtue of being instructed by the good sisters during the regular school terms. They had summer off.

There was sort of a hidden benefit to the grueling grind of going to summer school in July. It kept the kids on schedule with a daily routine that prevented any unnecessary ennui that afflicted both young and old when left without unregulated things to do and places to go. The human psyche is a strange piece of work indeed. We complain about regular and rigorous tasks equated with drudgery, but once freed from those obligations, we become quickly bored with unscheduled "free time" and yearn for the daily routine. Many an honest student, who feverishly anticipates the end of a school year, will readily admit that it is not long into the summer "vacation" that they secretly want to get back to school. There is truth in the philosophical awareness that there may, indeed, be more pleasure in *anticipating* a desired good than in the actual achieving of that good. This seems to be another example confusing the *means* and *ends* of life. People grouped together in that weird phenomenon called "society" somehow value accomplishments more than the process of acquiring. We think that we have to finish things, to get things—a job, a spouse, a home. We think that life will come to a happy and permanent end if we only had *fill in the blank*. There seems to be a disconnect between the individual desire for satisfaction in *doing* something and the societal pressures to *attain* something. Aided and abetted by economic needs for endless growth and supported by the created demands of advertising, the need to have things supersedes the process of life itself. Life is no longer in the living; it is in the attaining.

So there it is. Our public school probational Catholics did not have to worry about a long, hot, boring summer. They were still in the *process* of going to school. And there was a bit of relaxing fun about summer religious schools—even Sister St. Vincent seemed more relaxed and even eased up quite a bit on her threatening pocket clicker. Part of the fun was the arts and crafts sessions of the light summer curriculum. The kids—including the Sixth Avenue Wildcats—learned to make rather beautiful artifacts. They designed models of stained glass windows, built bird houses, made jewelry for their moms and leather eyeglass cases for their dads. There really was more emphasis on fun and less on religion—not that the boys associated religion with fun in the first place.

Tradition dictated that no summer school student showed up on the first day of class in July without the customary empty cigar box to be filled with all the supplies needed for the craft work. The boxes could be obtained at any store that sold cigars and cigarettes, which were too many to count in this World War II era of the 1940s and early '50s. The Wildcats claimed empty cigar box privileges from McCoy's corner pharmacy that was the nearest to the boys' home. Old Mr. McCoy was a gentle old soul whom apparently God created at a very advanced age behind the counter of his store from the beginning of time. The store was distinguished by its huge, oversized apothecary cylinders that filled the front window, giving the store the aura of holding secret medicinal powers that might convey the very ageless immortality enjoyed by its owner. On entering the store, one encountered a not unpleasant ethereal aroma suggesting both a hospital and a far-off land of exotic lotions and talcum.

Ageless Mr. McCoy knew all the boys. Each would readily volunteer for the errand of having a prescription filled at the store. The kindly pharmacist would invite the boy to read a comic book while waiting for the prescription to be filled. Prior glances at the wire magazine rack containing the treasured magazines evoked a thin smile on the old man's face as he proffered the invitation to share the adventures of Superman or Captain Marvel or Batman. Billy acknowledged that if one waited politely and quietly while waiting for the prescription, Mr. McCoy would allow the boy to have the book—for nothing! Take it home without paying!

Ageless Mr McCoy was the first owner of this corner drugstore where the boys bought their comic books. Courtesy of Jack & Brian Coll

The Wildcats were experts on the literature of comic books. Most of them learned how to read from these super heroic adventure stories. The colorful magazines cost ten cents—one liberty head dime. And it was no trivial matter to earn money for a monthly purchase of a new comic book. The boys had ingeniously devised a sort of comic book co-op in which they would each purchase a different magazine and then, after reading the book of choice, would trade with another boy. In this way, one had access to as many as ten comic books each month and only spending one thin dime! There was no formal plan to this system. Most books were read on rainy days when it was impossible to play baseball in their homemade league. And not every boy read at the same speed or cared for the books with the same concern. For example, no one wanted to trade with Ernie. His books always had a dank odor, as if they were rained on or left in a damp basement too long or, perhaps, had been handled too long by perspiring human hands.

"Geez, Ernie, how could you mess up a good book in less than a month?"

Another interesting fact revealed by the trading of comics was the different aesthetic appeal shown by each boy. Big Joe preferred Superman comics, and he would invariable purchase those books. Gussie liked the folksy comedy of Archie and his friends. Several of the boys wondered why Billy would prefer Batman to Superman, and these rainy-day conversations often resulted in critical reviews of the comic book industry. Unwittingly, the boys would compare the literary merit of their choices disguised in the youthful banter of their talk. Usually, it started with daring make-believe challenges of who was the better hero and how each would fare if they were engaged in combat with each other instead of their mortal foes in the book.

Big Joe's preference of Superman rested in the hero's indomitable power and strength. No one could ever beat Superman. Billy protested that this is precisely why he preferred Batman and his sidekick Robin. They were human—subject to pain and suffering and, God forbid, could even die! Batman and the Boy Wonder had to rely on their human ingenuity. Maybe they could not "fly faster than a speeding bullet," but they rode in the Batmobile—a souped-up futuristic car that every boy could imagine much easier than someone flying like bullets. Maybe Batman could not "jump tall buildings in a single bound," but he had his trusty bat kit, which produced a lanyard necessary to scale any building. Billy unknowingly was a literary realist. He eschewed the fantasy and symbolism of Superman. He preferred a hero who had to think his way out of a life-threatening jam. Big Joe was a romantic who wanted his heroes far above the limits of mere mortality. Each boy knew what he liked and was pretty good at explaining their relative artistic positions.

Today, however, the boys were more interested in empty cigar boxes, which the wise Mr. McCoy put away during the winter months when he knew the boys of summer school would be looking for the treasured boxes to carry their summer school supplies. It was a tradition that was passed on for years. Summer school supplies were kept in empty cigar boxes and the box of preference—God only knows why—were boxes previously filled with King Edward cigars.

The heat of the summer slipped by easily in the cool church hall. Attendance was mandatory, but the experience not totally unpleasant. Religious dogma was not the predominant part of the curriculum. There were lots of arts and crafts projects, justifying the reason for the King Edward cigar boxes, and the two Sisters of St. Joseph who faithfully walked the short five blocks from the more established and affluent Irish parish seemed less intimidating in their summer white habits. They too seemed to enjoy the more relaxed climate of a school with less rules and more fun. It was summer after all, and even the semi-pagan Catholics with no parochial school of their own—subject to the vile temptations of an entire public school year—needed a respite from the articles of faith.

The sisters as well as the school kids looked forward to the special treat that awaited them at the end of July when summer school ended—an all-day outing to Willow Grove Amusement Park. Willow Grove was the premier amusement park of the day, with rides galore and swimming and boating and picnicking. One's measure of wealth at Willow Grove was determined by how many tickets were purchased at the main gate. The tickets for the various venues were dispensed in long strips, which were carefully folded and pocketed in significant bulges until needed at the entrance to the rides. The most popular—costing five whole tickets per ride—and the most daring ride of all was the Thunderbolt—the fearful roller coaster of all roller coasters. One's courage (and wealth) was gauged by how many times you rode on the Thunderbolt! Many a summer school kid, after ignoring the warnings from vigilant parents not to ride too soon after eating, disgorged their picnic lunches somewhere between halfway and final terminus of the Thunderbolt ride. The parents were more embarrassed than the youngsters whenever lunch went flying from the heights of the roller coaster. In fact, such regurgitate events became future points of pride among the members of Reds's gang. *Wildcats* on the *Thunderbolt* were fitting similes for daring deeds of bravery, and up-chucking on the ride merely enhanced one's reputation for fearlessness.

The trip to Willow Grove Park was a ritualistic ending of the summer religious school experience, and pretty much ended formal summer activities for the youngsters. August languished in the summer heat when air conditioning meant no more than portable fans with which a lucky few, living in stifling row homes, could simply blow hot air from one corner of the room to the other. There might be a rare day-trip to the New Jersey seashore—usually Atlantic City—but few families had automobiles. Most of the dads worked at mills and plants that were in walking distance from home. Lengthy vacations were not in the economic picture of these hardworking but financially challenged people. It is safe to say that many of the Wildcat players never travelled more than a few miles from home, and no one ever questioned the simplicity of their uncomplicated culture.

The boys of the Sixth Avenue Wildcats played ball during the hot days of August—much to the chagrin of their moms who warned them against becoming "overheated" and risking the dreaded disease of infantile paralysis. No one called it polio then, and Jonas Salk was years away from eradicating this fearsome disease. The boys were a bit sobered when Big Joe's cousin contracted polio and was left with a withered right arm that hung useless by his side for the rest of his life. Mothers thought that their warnings were now justified, but the boys played anyway—no matter how hot the weather. It seemed that polio and the Thunderbolt were in the same category of life's risks.

Chapter Nine

A Centennial Celebration

E veryone loves a good party. And what could be better than a week-long party thrown by a town celebrating the hundredth anniversary of its incorporation. This was a big deal for the small town. Funds were appropriated and a special centennial committee formed to plan and oversee a great pageant depicting special historic moments in the town's one hundred years of existence. The pageantry would unfold on the town's athletic field, a football arena of hallowed memories of local high school and semi-professional football greats, many of whom were older relatives of the boys of Sixth Avenue.

In addition to the pantomimed pageantry, there would be parades and nightly fireworks for a whole week. Local merchants decorated their shops for the occasion. Red, white, and blue bunting adorned the stores in the three-block "down town" shopping area. Men grew the obligatory centennial beards for the occasion, and commemorative wooden nickels became an approved form of mercenary exchange to honor the special anniversary.

The townsfolk were genuinely proud of their community. It is a true paradigm of small-town America. Late 1600 deeds show the purchase of land by William Penn himself. Subsequent transactions by industrious Quakers made the one-square-mile borough a thriving river town, rich in limestone quarries and iron ore, which would eventually yield iron and steel mills. A convenient river hugged the southern boundary of the town, affording easy transportation of manufactured goods. The landed gentry saw the town's population increase with the gradual influx of immigrants from Western Europe. Laborers from Ireland, Poland, Italy, Germany, and the Scandinavian countries filled the factories and mills and quarries with a cheap labor that provided sustenance for the immigrants and profit for the town.

The signature event of the celebration was to be the reenactment of the Battle of Matson's Ford, which took place in the early days of our nation's fight for independence. Peter Matson, in 1741, had purchased land at the river's edge where a bend in the river provided a natural crossing for goods and people to the other side of the river. Matson's Ford was the one name that all townsfolk could relate to history. It was across this very ford that General Lafayette led two thousand colonial troops in a daring escape from the British. The main street of town, to this day, bears the name of this French ally of America.

In December of that same year, 1777, George Washington was moving his colonial army to the safer confines of Valley Forge while the British under the command of William Howe were comfortably settled in Philadelphia. A redcoat foraging party encountered a band of colonial soldiers laying down a wagon pontoon bridge across the Schuylkill River at Matson's Ford. The skirmish was brief with Washington's men falling back across the river while destroying their makeshift bridge. The British foraged elsewhere while the colonials made their way to their frigid winter quarters at Valley Forge.

Matson's Ford Bridge across the Schuylkill River where the boys reenacted the battle with the Redcoats. C. 1900 Courtesy of Jack & Brian Coll

While history remembers more of the Valley Forge encampment and says not much of the skirmish at the river, our young boys would rectify that slight by participating in "The Battle of Matson's Ford" as part of the pageant celebrating the town's birthday. They will reenact the battle on the athletic field for five consecutive nights, with the boys uniformed as authentic colonials, replete in tricorne hats and fictitious ramrod muskets, portraying a heroic retreat from the river while the redcoats tried not overact their role of victorious invaders.

But first there had to be rehearsals. Two weeks before the big celebration, the boys would line up outside the school in their gym outfits (white shorts and tee shirts). The plan was to march the six blocks from the local high school to the community athletic field where the great pageantry would be played out in pantomime in just two short weeks. There seemed to be a special urgency on the part of faculty advisors who were trying to herd the energetic adolescents into two neat rows. Their goal was to march the boys up the main street of town to the football field. The road—the main street of town—is the very same avenue that the Marquis de Lafayette marched his weary American troops out of harm's way from the villainous redcoats.

Mr. Henry Ryba, Billy's homeroom teacher, was especially anxious to have his boys show a bit of decorum and dignity as the boys were to be passing by an inquisitive gaggle of shoppers and other assortments of towns people who happened upon the street this day. Granted it is expecting much of ninth grade boys to appreciate the dignity and solemnity of celebrating the Battle of Matson's Ford. The names of Washington, Lafayette, and Peter Matson were not nearly as familiar or relevant as Abbot and Costello, Joe DiMaggio, or Tarzan. What was important to the boys is the fact that they were being let out of school early and going to the athletic field in the very attire that shouted out FUN. They were wearing their gymnasium attire. They had on the very clothing that suggested movement, activity, running, jumping, tumbling—in a word, all the activities that one did in Gym class. The exception, of course, was that this was not gym class. The boys were out in public, in the middle of the street, herded into the semblance of a marching line of soldiers who were expected to act with grace, dignity, and discipline that reflected the values of the very high school that nurtured these boys and the very high school where Henry Ryba taught.

Poor Mr. Ryba. The sight of his precious charges acting like silly children—making faces at each other, punching arms, gyrating arms and legs in perpetual motion—was too much for him to bear as passing townspeople gave sideway glances of disapproval at the errant adolescents. Finally, he screamed above the noise of the boisterous boys, "Don't you boys have any self-respect!" Silence. Mr. Ryba's homeroom class simultaneously stopped talking and stopped moving. The sudden cessation of horseplay was due more to the unexpected tone and outrage of Mr. Ryba's commanding question rather than any understanding of what he meant. The boys had no idea of what "self-respect" meant. They intuitively grasped the dire meaning of Henry Ryba's supreme dismay with them. They sensed, as a pet animal senses from a prohibitive command of its master, that certain actions are not meeting with approval. There is a compounded feeling—somewhere between innocence and guilt, that they must be doing something wrong, but cannot imagine what it is. Similar effects are realized when a fearful parent warns a tiny child not to touch a hot stove. "Don't touch that stove!" the parent screams, and the innocent child experiences a strange feeling of dread that is a necessary precondition of human freedom. The child does not know the parent wants to prevent him from being painfully burned. Yet the child has never experienced the touch of a hot stove, and the child has not yet actually touched this stove. Still the command is so dire sounding that the child feels guilty—about being innocent. It is a strange lesson in the possibilities that accompany human freedom. *Now* the child knows, from the unintelligible command, that it is possible to act freely from internal psychological restraints. He intuits from the dreadful sound of the parent's warning, that if he *ought* not touch that damn stove, he *can* touch it if he wants, in spite of the parent's command. The brat has learned an oblique lesson in human freedom.

Again, we have a wrong-headed adult lesson in human freedom and possibilities. No one faults the parent for the sudden and explosive action in order to prevent harm to the child. The parent, in some way, is as innocent as the child. It plays out like a Greek tragedy—no one is to blame, yet a lesson is learned the hard way. In this case, the child "learns" to act with blind obedience to a harsh command that begins a process of resentment for authority that restricts one's freedom. Can Oedipus be far behind? And of course, the whole transaction is for the good of the child.

What the boys of the centennial pageant should have learned is the meaning of Mr. Ryba's lament. "Don't you boys have any self-respect!" He wanted the boys to have more pride in themselves. He wanted them to know that they were worth more than making fools of themselves in public. He wanted them to know that pride is a virtue not a vice. Henry Ryba thinks the boys should have had more pride in themselves than to let the proud elders of their home town think they were a bunch of silly kids without a serious thought in their heads.

The boys, however, had a pretty good idea of their own individual worth. They had proven that many times on the baseball field in their own made-up league, away from the judgmental eyes of adults. They got down to the business of celebrating the centennial—in their own time—and put on a great pageant for the townspeople. The Battle of Matson's Ford was never performed better. In fact, if one discounted history, one could swear the redcoats were defeated.

Chapter Ten

The Second Greatest Generation

Tom Brokaw dubbed the generation of brave Americans who fought through both the Great Depression and the horrors of World War II as the greatest generation. And rightly so. Not since the civil war had America's existence as a nation been so severely challenged. The depths of poverty, starvation, destitution, homelessness, class divisions, all have been dutifully documented as horrific conditions of the Great Depression. The economic price of climbing out from those years of misery was in great part due to employment in the mills, mines, and factories needed to produce the military means of defeating the World War II Axis.

The parents of Reds and his buddies were part of that great generation. They fought the Depression and the war—and America was a better place because of their immense sacrifices. They first fought starvation at home and fought a fierce enemy abroad. The accomplishments of those stalwart people can never be exaggerated.

The children of those brave people were not exempt from the struggle and sacrifices of those twin terrors of economic and military power. They were old enough to know and experience the horrors but not old enough to be directly involved in the fight. They were mature enough to be afraid but too young to alter the results. They were time-fated bystanders who were engaged in two of the greatest social calamities of human history that were not of their making. Nevertheless, they have a story to tell about surviving the brutal realities of the mid-twentieth century. The boys of the Sixth Avenue Wildcats were part of that generation. They are the second greatest generation.

Billy was born in a third-floor apartment that his mother and father rented from a neighbor they knew. The Depression had only begun when he was born and his father lost his job at a local mill. Billy never knew why he lost his job, but he remembers well how his mother bitterly reminded his dad that it was his temper that got him into trouble at a time when jobs were disappearing faster than ice cubes in the summer.

His dad would claim that his boss had engaged in name-calling and had spoken a word that no self-respecting man should take without reprisal. Billy never knew what that epithet was—perhaps an ethnic slur. Billy's dad was not yet a citizen and was working hard at becoming a good American by first losing his Italian accent. Regardless, his dad was out of work, and there was rent to pay to shelter baby Billy and his four-year-old sister and mother. The owner of the house was a *paisan*—a skilled stone mason who had work and assured Billy's dad that he would not evict him, and that he knew of his honesty and would be re-paid when things got better. Billy grew up learning all these horror stories of the Great Depression, of hunger, loss of employment, and eviction. There were also gratifying stories—how a friendly milkman left a bottle of milk on the doorsteps, how friends and relatives pulled together to help others in their time of great need. He grew up knowing the meaning of need and effort and anxiety. He knew how his parents worried constantly over money, over the basic necessities of life. He was a kid growing up, but he knew. And he knew because he was part of the equation that was the depression. He may not have been a direct player in response to the travails of the time, but nevertheless he *was* a player. He took on odd jobs of taking trash out for his neighbors using a wagon to haul weekly garbage to the "town dump," which was conveniently located for him right down the back ally from the rented home he lived in. On Saturdays, he would sanitize that wagon and wait outside of the new Atlantic & Pacific supermarket and wheel home bags of groceries for the housewives who shopped there. Twenty-five cents a bag was a good deal! The kids of the second greatest generation learned never to waste anything because they did not have much in the first place. This trait explains their industry in obtaining their meager baseball equipment by selling old papers and repairing their bats and balls with screws and tape.

It was not easy for them growing up as Depression kids—physically and mentally. Big Joe's family found themselves strapped during one of the Depression day Christmases and could not afford colored lights for their tree. Big Joe found some clear lights that someone had discarded and had the ingenious idea of painting them with his sister's nail polish. The final product wasn't bad and the tree was adorned with red lights. The project served a double purpose when Joe fulfilled an essay requirement for his English teacher at school. He wrote a story about a very poor family who could not afford colored Christmas lights for their tree and painted clear lights they found in the trash with nail polish. Each student had to read their essays aloud to the entire class, and when Big Joe finished, his teacher, Mrs. Guest, asked with kind, but misguided sympathy, "Joseph, is that a true story?" Mortified beyond belief, Big Joe muttered a hanging head denial and swore that he had made it up with no basis in reality. Big Joe knew that the entire class knew and that he was exposed with the great indignity of being poor. To compound his misery, he would have to consider further humiliation by confessing to the priest on Saturday that he had lied to his teacher and to the entire class. Not a big deal, adults might think. But they would be wrong. It was a big deal.

The second generation Depression kids did not cause the Depression. They were completely innocent of those who played the economic market games and created the horrendous vagaries of instability that made innocent victims of so many people. The kids were even more vulnerable because of their youth and inability to control their own destiny. Yet like their parents, they struggled through in their own unobserved kid ways—unnoticed by well-meaning adults who were so preoccupied with their own problems that they took the kids for granted and never saw that they were struggling as hard as the adults without any means of influencing the social powers that controlled them.

It was the same regarding World War II. No one noticed how much the second generation kids were affected by the war. Gussie's older brother was a paper boy who delivered the *Philadelphia Evening Bulletin* every afternoon after school. Gussie remembered when his brother delivered the news of Pearl Harbor. He was certainly old enough to know that this was deadly news. Subsequent news headlines struck fear into the heart of any American citizen as the Japanese imperial army conquered great expansion of territory in the South Pacific. What was reported in the papers was confirmed at the Riant and Forest theaters where benign films of Abbott and Costello were replaced by Hollywood's propaganda films depicting the fall of island after island to the brutal Japanese forces— Bataan, Guadalcanal, the

Solomon Islands, Corregidor, all of the Philippines. Saturday after Saturday, the boys witnessed the horrors of war—at the movies.

They all had close relatives fighting on both fronts now in Europe and the South Pacific. Older brothers, uncles, cousins, neighbors—no one was exempt. The kids could draw only one conclusion from all the reports of Japanese conquests at the beginning of the war. They thought they were going to be invaded and conquered right here on Sixth Avenue just as the islanders were in the movies. There were daily air raid drills in school when the bell would ring in the middle of class and the kids were shepherded into the musty whitewashed walls of the basement. There were weekly air raid drills at night when the fire siren wailed its warning for all household lights to be extinguished and curtains drawn so that no light could be spotted by the deadly bombers of the German Luftwaffe. No real raids came, of course, but the kids weren't sure—neither were the adults. All signs indicated that we were losing the war, and when there were reports of German U-boats spotted off the New Jersey coast, well, it took a great deal of courage to keep on going—for kids as well as adults.

Food was rationed. Billy would go to the corner store for his mom with blue tokens that would limit the number of canned goods a family could buy. Twenty cents for a can of peas and one blue token. Red tokens rationed out the amount of fresh meat one could buy—and the meat was second grade to begin with. The people of the home front knew that all good things went to the armed forces in the military theaters scattered worldwide. Gasoline was rationed with stamps that each family received—the amount determined by the type of job you had and the distance one had to travel. If one had to drive to work at a defense factory, then more gas stamps were issued.

Every member of the Sixth Avenue Wildcats learned how to roll cigarettes—purportedly for their fathers who could not buy quality cigarettes. The best-grade tobacco became cigarettes for the soldiers, sailors, and marines. What appeared to be tobacco droppings swept up from the floor of the curing rooms was sold in little bags and then delicately poured into special papers which one sealed shut with just the right amount of spit from one's tongue. The boys became adept tobacconists at this homemade method of making cigarettes. They were good at helping out in many ways on the home front. They would search out crumpled discarded cigarette packs and peel off the tinfoil inner lining that had secured the freshness of the tobacco. The silver foil would be wrapped around an ever-increasing ball of silver destined to be given to the war-effort redemption site and miraculously converted into guns or bullets or God knows what. The boys knew only that their efforts were helping beat the Nazis and the Japs. Collecting silver linings from cigarette packs was simply a more exotic task than redeeming old bottles and cans and newspapers. The boys competed among themselves by claiming the biggest and heaviest silver ball to take to the war effort center.

"Hungry and unemployed, millions sought relief in soup lines during the Great Depression"

The sorrows of the war felt by this younger generation were mostly unnoticed by the adults. They lost uncles and older brothers and neighbors. They stood silently by their parents at funerals for the dead heroes who returned in flag-draped caskets. The boys may have been too young to fight in the war, but they were old enough to know and fear what was happening. Perhaps their youthful bravado was exaggerated when they emerged from the movies staging make-believe fights with the enemy, but there was a sobering awareness of the horrors of the war when they huddled in the bomb shelters or attended the funerals of their fallen relatives.

Ernie came to school one day carrying the helmet worn by his uncle Georgie who fought in the infantry in the South Pacific. The helmet had a small hole near the top and a huge jagged hole on the other side where the bullet exited. Ernie's uncle had been rendered unconscious by the exploding shell, but the inner lining of the helmet had allowed enough room at the top to have the bullet pass above his head. Georgie was one of the lucky ones and the boys silently absorbed that fact as they quietly passed the helmet to each other.

The radio was the focal point of family life during the World War II years. The radio was the source of information and entertainment. Families would gather around the living room radio to listen faithfully to their favorite programs—comedy shows like *Jack Benny* and *Bob Hope*; spooky, scary shows like *The Inner Sanctum* and *The Shadow*; ethnic favorites like *Molly Goldberg* and *Life with Luigi*. A Monday night favorite was *Lux Presents Hollywood* when a current motion picture would be scripted for an hour radio show with the actual movie stars reading the re-enacted movie live from Radio City Music Hall. It was a tribute to the human imagination, which transformed America's living room into a movie theater. Imagine, listening to a movie—on the radio! Maybe that was the source of creativity and leadership of this second greatest generation. Things were not spelled out to them in black and white. Reality was nuanced. Just as they had to imagine and create their own baseball league, so they had to imagine their way out of depression's poverty with homemade colored Christmas tree lights and pretend combat with the enemy axis on Saturday afternoon at the movies. The radio, before television and the internet, provided instant reality in living color, offered a medium that allowed the imagination to expand into myriad possibilities of new places and new ideas. And without ever knowing it, this youthful generation was shaped around that source of creativity.

The radio was also an important dispenser of news, especially news about the war. Daily newspapers and weekly newsreels at the movie houses also served that role, but in the days before instant tweeting and texting, it took time for the printed and celluloid news to reach the general population. The radio then was the analog to instant messaging now. The second greatest generation kids can never forget the tinny voice of Edward R. Murrow crackling over the shortwave band as he reported live from London as that city was mercilessly bombed by the German Luftwaffe. "This is London." And every anxious listener on the other side of the radio knew what that meant. And many a second-generation kid sat next to their grandmother or aunt and watched their eyes tear as Gabriel Heatter, another favorite newscaster, began his nightly war time news with his patent opener, "There is good news tonight." Billy's aunt had three sons in the war, and there was a severe shortage of "good news" especially in the early years of the war. Billy was present when a telegram came to his aunt's house and watched as she opened the message with trembling fingers. Telegrams were not good things for families to receive during the war. This, however, was a thoughtful message from one of her sons who wished her a happy Mother's Day two weeks in advance. He was shipping out for duty on a destroyer escort mission somewhere in the North Atlantic and knew he would be out of contact for a long while. Billy was mature enough to know that his aunt's fear was not transformed into joy, but rather a confused sense of relief. And Billy shared her confusion.

A popular radio that united families in information and entertainment was the Stromberg-Carlson console model. The 440 model with AM and shortwave frequencies was something of a status symbol for blue-collar families of the second greatest generation youngsters. Needless to say, those who "owned" one did so with easy credit and a friend who worked at Sears, Roebuck & Company. Who would not be impressed with this electronic wonder-soul embodied in a stately cabinet of walnut veneer and its enclosed "Acoustical Labyrinth" speaker—the very cutting edge of audio transmission. The shortwave band was the *piece de resistance* of modern technology with hundreds of stations to carry listeners to remote parts of the globe. Unfortunately, for Gussie's father who was born in Abruzzi, the shortwave vacuum tube of their proud possession radio was confiscated by the local authorities. Gussie's father, after all, was not too far from being an "alien." He was a naturalized citizen—proudly exchanging his Italian name of "Vincenzo" to the less romantic but more American sobriquet "Vincent." The fact that Vince worked hard to rid himself of his "foreign" accent, that he was a defense worker during the war, that he proudly flew an American flag from his front yard flag pole that he had placed in the ground himself, that he had no memory of Italy, which he left when he was a mere five-year-old boy traveling with his mother and father—none of these facts seemed to matter. Italy was on the wrong side in this war, and Vincent was on the wrong side of the world. The family never mentioned this embarrassing event of having to surrender a valuable part of such a valuable commodity. It was like losing a part of one's body. Worst of all was the shame and indignity of even suggesting that somehow this family was not as American as everyone else. Gussie's youthful innocence, and wisdom, tried to ameliorate the humiliation by jokingly suggesting that maybe the government feared that "Pop would communicate with Mussolini." It was only long after the war ended that his father could appreciate Gussie's humor—and his wisdom.

World War II mercifully ended, but five short years later, the human insanity of war returned on the Korean Peninsula. It was at this time and on this occasion that this generation lost its imagination and creativity. The unnoticed generation of the Great Depression and the Great War were now directly and forcefully involved in an unnoticed war—a war that historians only guess at the number of causalities, and no one seemed to care. The Sixth Avenue wildcats had lost their innocence. They were all grown up. They were adults.

Chapter Eleven

Billy's Notebook Part II: A Farmer Looks at War

*B*illy's father had come from Italy as a young boy with his father, mother, and older brother, Luigi. After ten years of subsistence farming in what was then rural Pennsylvania, the mother, father, and brother returned to Italy to recover an old farmhouse they left there. Billy's dad never saw his parents again, and his brother was caught there with the outbreak of WWII. Luigi returned to the States after the war as "Lou" and took a job driving a truck in Patterson, New Jersey. Billy looked forward to Uncle Louie's visits every Sunday when he would recount to Billy what it was like living under the threat of the Nazis who had taken over their farmhouse as their headquarters. On Sunday, after the traditional noontime dinner, Uncle Louie would tell pieces of his story until it was time to turn on the Stromberg Carlson radio and listen to the opera—live from the Met. Louie had a limited formal education—ten years in the United States—but he spoke perfect English—and knew his opera. Billy's notebook had a detailed account of his uncle's amazing experiences, told in Uncle Louie's voice, as Billy had remembered it.*

On September 1, 1939, when Hitler's crushing Panzer Divisions blitz-krieged into Poland and plunged the world into its bloody war, I was more concerned about the price of olives. I was content with my wife and family of seven children on my small farm in Faicchio, a small town in the province of Benevento, just south of Naples. The rest of the world could take its shortcut to hell if it chose, but pigs, cows, goats, figs, olives, and cheese were more my concern. I was a farmer, and a farmer has the distinct privilege of living in a secure world of his own. At least this was true in the old days, and it was true for me in 1939 when there was no milkman, but our own cows; no bread deliveries, but our own outside hearths, which always smelled sweet and pure with fresh baked bread. When we wanted bacon, we slaughtered a hog. The milk from the goats provided us with butter and cheese. Olive oil came readily from our small grove of olive trees; grapes, raisins, and wine came from the same vines; and the chickens laid eggs. Potatoes, corn, wheat, melons, spinach, beans, and carrots— not a superabundance but enough for the extended family that included Mom and Pop. We were a self-sufficient family on our own land, living from our own labor, and to hell with the rest of the world. That was the philosophy of the farmer of old, and it was my philosophy when the global war began in 1939.

Four years later, in September of 1943, the invasion of Italy at Salerno by American troops exploded our rural indifference to war and made realists of us all. Shortly before the invasion, the Italian troops under Marshall Badoglio surrendered to the Allies, and only those under the brutal Fascist leader Rodolfo Graziani continued to give armed resistance to Mark Clark's Fifth Army, which was slowly but surely creeping up the boot of Italy. In a matter of weeks, the war was at our front door. By day, German tanks and armored cars went clanking down the dirt lane past our house, moving to offer resistance to the advancing Americans. By night, American artillery fire rocked and rumbled Mount Vitolano where a front was formed about five miles south of us. Advancing Germans rushing to the front were little concerned about Italian farmers, but a few weeks later, hungry retreating Germans were to be feared. Rumors went buzzing through our small village about German infantry men stripping the land of edibles—chickens, pigs, calves—anything that could be carried or put into trucks. What was worse, and proved to be my biggest fear, was the report that able-bodied Italian men were being forced to work or even fight for the Germans as they retreated north. Stories of abducted Italian women were not uncommon either. I learned quickly that war was hell.

About one week prior to the Germans retreating through our village, American planes dropped leaflets prepared under the supervision of Marshal Badoglio. The leaflet urged all the townspeople to hide all foodstuffs, clothing, and other items that the retreating Germans might seek and arm ourselves with shotguns and rifles and flee to the nearby mountains. Several days later, I was aroused from sleep at one in the morning by a neighbor's cry that "the Germans are coming!" With the help of my wife Theresa and my two oldest boys—Joseph who was fourteen and Tony, twelve—I hid all our clothing and food in a huge brick oven, which we camouflaged with branches and dirt. My wife and I assembled our seven children—the youngest, Albert, was only five months old and prepared to leave for my father-in-law's cottage about five miles away in a mountainous area. We would spend the first night in caves in the mountains to see if it were possible to move safely on from there. Amid all the confusion of packing and calming crying children, there was one other unexpected element of delay. My father, age seventy-one, refused to leave.

"But, Pop," I argued, "you can't stay here."

"And why not?" he answered blandly. "It's my house. Besides what could *i Tedeschi* do to an old man like me?" It was no use. Once Pop made up his mind, that was it. And if Pop would stay, then Mom, age seventy, would stay also. There was nothing I could do to convince them to leave the house, and with the Germans practically in our wheat fields, I had no time to argue. It was with a sad heart that I left the house that night.

Despite all the horror and panic of that night and the weeks that followed, the meeting of Pop and the German soldiers is so humorous that I must laugh whenever I call it to mind. Pop himself told me the story, and it was confirmed by a neighboring villager named Angelo who was hiding in the bushes nearby. Since our farmhouse was situated high above the town, it was one of the first sought by the Germans to use as a headquarters and as a vantage point to view approaching troops from the south. Shortly after I left for the mountains, fifteen German soldiers led by their captain climbed onto our wooden porch and tried to gain entrance through the window. Pop soon heard the noise, came running to the window, and in sharp Italian syllables scolded the closest German for trying to break the window. He proceeded to reproach all fifteen for endangering the security of the patio, which was creaking under their weight, and rebuked their ill manners for not entering a home in the proper way through the door. The mental picture of fifteen pillaging soldiers, like truant school boys caught in act of thievery, timidly climbing back down the porch at the command of a little old man, still brings a smile to my face. Smiles were hard to come by then.

The German captain, in excellent Italian, assured Pop that the visiting Germans would protect him from the advancing American "enemy who were pillaging the countryside." While he was calming my father's supposed fear of "ransacking Americans," his men found, killed, cleaned, and cooked the chickens I had left for Mom and Pop and were washing them down with Pop's best wine. The next morning, when German tanks came rattling through our fields ripping down our olive trees and grape vines and when German mortar men were despoiling our apple trees, which were bursting with the first week of October fruit, it was more than Pop could bear. He wisely decided to join me and the rest of the family farther up the mountain. Mom would leave first, he decided, and he would slip away when the Germans left on one of their many foraging parties. He nonchalantly walked among the Germans as he had done the night before so as not to arouse suspicion, and when his chance came, he sneaked off into the woods and joined me at my father-in-law's cottage.

"Where's Mom?" I asked quickly.

"Isn't she here?" my father answered. "She left eight hours before I did."

I seized my shot gun from the corner and dashed back into the woods. About halfway between our farmhouse and my in-law's place, I found Mom sitting on a log beside the road. She was weeping bitterly. My mother had misunderstood Pop's directions and thought she was supposed to meet him at this spot. She would not abandon her mistaken rendezvous and remained there for eight hours, even though she suspected that Pop was unsuccessful in his escape and was probably lying dead at the house. When I assured her that Pop was safe, she collapsed in my arms and I gently carried my seventy-year-old mother to my father-in-law's house.

My closest brush with the German soldiers came two days later when Pop prodded me into returning to the house to see what damage they had done. It was extremely difficult to make him understand that the Germans would not give me, a man of forty years, the same privileges of freedom they gave old people. I agreed to go back with him, but would wait and hide in the brush. If the house was empty, he was to wave his handkerchief at the door and I would join him inside. From the bushes, I could hear the soldiers busy at work throughout the town. The sounds of shovels and picks scraping the earth blended with the cursing and shouting of men carried a great distance in the quiet October air. The Germans occupying our house must have been among the others, for there was Pop furiously waving his big hanky at the side door. All things considered, the house was in pretty good condition. Pop complained that all his wine was gone, but I was happy to discover that the Germans had not found our hidden clothing and bedding in the outdoor oven. Not wanting to stretch my luck, I hurried my father through the house and was two steps out the door heading back to the woods when six young German soldiers came around the house and blocked my path. "Halt! Halt!" they shouted. I got panicky; and sweat broke out on my brow, my hands got cold and clammy, and my throat became knotted and dry. When their leader drew his service pistol, I stormed heaven with silent prayers. They marched us back into the house and began browsing around, all the while directing rapid fire questions at me in German. My limited knowledge of German and their total ignorance of both Italian and English made a difficult situation worse. Our fortune turned for the better when they started thumbing through a book that belonged to one of my boys. They came upon a picture of Marshall Badoglio, who had renounced Hitler, and promptly spat at it. But on the next page was a photo of Rodolfo Graziani, the Fascist and pro-Hitlerite who continued offering resistance to the US troops in Italy. This was my chance to work into their good graces. I interrupted their admiring comments of the Fascist leader and spoke out.

"Graziani, Gut, Gut!"

"Ich . . . in Afrika . . . Krieg." I was trying to tell them that I fought in Mussolini's Ethiopian campaign under Graziani. It is true that I was conscripted into the Italian army shortly after I returned to Italy with my parents from America. The war was over, however, and I served for a very brief period as record keeper in the quarter master unit. When one of the Germans gave me a skeptical shove, I produced a cheap bronze medal and accompanying document, which I received for my "Ethiopian Campaign" duties. Actually, these medals were a dime a dozen and were given to everyone who was drafted before or after the war. I had never fought under Graziani or with anyone else in that sordid effort of Mussolini to restore the Roman Empire. But I fooled the Germans, and gaining confidence, I repeated, "Graziani, Gut."

"Gut, Gut," they responded and gave me a friendly slap on the back.

It wasn't until I won their admiration that I appreciated the terrifying dilemma that had confronted me. If I had not feigned an undying devotion to Graziani, they might have shot me, but now I realized that I may have overplayed my hand and was expected to join them on the battlefield. I was truly out of the pot and into the proverbial frying pan. Just then, however, they were distracted by gun fire not far from the house and ran off, leaving me and Pop alone. We quickly fled from the house and returned to our mountain sanctuary.

I record these events as some kind of miraculous Providence and Guidance during these terrible months of suffering and grief of all of the people of Faicchio.

On the morning of October 13, 1943, the brilliant sunlight of southern Italy and the heavy artillery of advancing American troops exploded simultaneously against the fair hillsides of our town. The GI's were throwing everything at the retreating Germans. But Faicchio presented problems. Nestled between Mount Erbano and Mount Acire, its narrow passes could be held by a few German rear-guard guns. The Americans split their forces around each of the mountains in an effort to squeeze the enemy in a pincer. Almost a week before the fighting began in our area, the entire town had moved back into the mountains. I assumed logistical leadership of the one hundred villagers and with twenty other men set up a camp-site in a deep gorge halfway up the mountain. The gorge protected us from stray artillery fire.

With picks and shovels, we dug caves into the sides of this narrow valley, and having cut down several huge trees, we placed them across the entrance to the gorge. When all was in readiness, the rest of the people came—more than one hundred men, women, and children—a human caravan carrying beds, mattresses, small stoves, pots, and pans, driving before them cows, goats, pigs, cats, and dogs. They tried to take what was necessary for them to have and what would be advantageous if the Germans had them.

For two days and nights the earth trembled as heavy artillery and mortar fire shook the ground. We were safe from the direct line of the shells, but were endangered by flying shrapnel, which could come ripping in from any angle. My brother-in-law, Pasquale Massaro, was wounded by shrapnel on October 14. He was returning up the mountainside bearing sad news for me and my family. From his position on the slope, which gave him a good view of the entire village beneath us, he had seen that our farmhouse was bombed to the ground. He actually witnessed fourteen American twin engine planes returning to their base after bombing and strafing German supply lines just north of Faicchio. As they flew over our home, the Germans from within the house opened up against them with machine gun fire. Four of the planes peeled out of formation, circled back, and leveled the house. In a matter of minutes, our home was a smoking rubble. My father was inconsolable. I was thankful that the house was all we lost. My mother, father, wife, and seven children came through this nightmare unharmed.

October 15, the feast day of St. Theresa of Avila, was another beautiful sunlit morning. The firing had stopped the night before, and I was returning from the spring with water buckets when I saw five soldiers walking through the meadow below. Their long trench coats led me to believe our mountain hideaway was about to be set upon by the starving Germans, but the leggings and foot gear of the five were different from those of the Germans. A closer look confirmed the best of what I had hoped for. They were American soldiers! I dropped the buckets and ran down to the meadow shouting to them. We were free! On October 15, 1943, on the feast of the Carmelite Saint of Avila, we were free! Since I spoke perfect English, they thought I was one of their spies still in disguise as an Italian farmer, but I quickly explained that I had spent ten years in the States and was educated there.

The days that followed were in marked contrast to the previous weeks of sneaking through the woods and digging in the mountain. It took a few days to walk about freely without fear of being forced to fight or labor for the Germans. But a quick glimpse of our shattered countryside soon made us aware that this was a time for reconstruction. The fields that autumn had not been harvested with sickles and scythes, but rather with howitzers and mortars. Lack of food was our biggest problem. The GIs who occupied Faicchio were a tremendous help to us. They supplied us with all sorts of food—flour, sugar, salt. Their resourcefulness was inexhaustible, and we would have been licked without them. In an effort to repay their kindness and generosity, I did some reconnaissance work, riding out with them in their jeeps and pointing out the hills and mountains I knew so well.

But soon they had to move on in pursuit of the Germans and continue to fight what must have seemed to them to be an endless war. I had made friends with quite a few of the American boys who had helped us—Capt. Paul Stefano, from Ridley Park, Pennsylvania; the Kelly brothers, Sgt. Lou and Cpl. Dick who teamed up on anti-aircraft half-track; Capt. Jones, Capt. Shumaker, and a score of others with whom I had grown friendly. Eventually they all left us and we turned to the work of cleaning up. We were farmers and there was farming to be done. What could be salvaged of the autumn cops must be harvested and winter crops had to be planted. For us the war was over. Only the scars remained.

Since our farmhouse was a causality of the bombing raids, our immediate obstacle was housing, which was quickly hurdled even though it meant temporarily splitting up our family. An elderly couple whose only son was a prisoner of war in Russia gladly opened their door to some of us, and since the weather was perfect—it hadn't rained in a month—I slept outside under the stars for most of the time. The days would find me, Pop, and the boys dividing our time between fixing the house and planting the fields.

One warm day in mid-November, we were sitting next to our ruined house eating lunch when we detected a foul odor in the air. This prompted Pop to ask if any of the cats or dogs were missing. A quick check found no missing pets, but there was no doubt of the pungent smell of death and decay. After lunch, we noticed a swarm of large horse-flies buzzing around the rubble of an entire wall that had been caved in and reasoned that there lay the source of our mysterious odor. Grabbing our picks, Pop and I began at opposite ends, pulling away debris in a playful race to the center of the pile of stone. When I reached the spot where the flies were swarming furiously, I picked away a large piece of plaster and uncovered a pair of German boots. Further uncovering increased the intensity of the odor so greatly that my eyes began to water. Finally, we pulled away the last stone and the mystery was solved. It was a dead German, half rotted away, lying face down, his bony fingers still gripping a machine gun. It was a ghastly sight. Three rounds of ammunition were at his side with only five shots fired, and a Luger pistol was holstered about his waist. When I cut the belt loose with a sickle, the pistol slid to the ground, and a large bewildered maggot slithered out of the barrel. The horrible scene called for an iron stomach, which I did not possess. This was the final chapter of our war story. The last grim reminder of the horrors of battle.

It was a war that invaded the sacred, sheltered life of a farmer, indifferent to war but forced to be otherwise. It was a war that turned yellow fields of wheat into churned quagmires of mud and stone—and sometimes blood. It was a war that forced me to leave my home and seek refuge like an animal in the mountains, in constant fear for myself and my family. A war that eventually destroyed our home and devastated our livelihood, and now, lest I forget that war, I find buried under the ruins of my own home a scene that tells in stronger language than words the horror of war. That ghastly image remains with me as a lasting reminder that I stared war in the face. I didn't like what I saw.

Billy's Grandfather and Grandmother in an undated photo on their hillside farm in southern Italy. The farmhouse was taken over by the Germans in World War II.

Chapter Twelve

Vita Mutatur, Non Tollitur

At what point in life does one become aware of his or her mortality? Cute anecdotal stories suggest that this momentous event occurs somewhere in childhood with the death of a pet. Little Emma's parents convince her that her dear goldfish, Finny, is going to his or her(?) Eternal Reward and that the ceremonial burial at sea (a handy toilet serves as a ready surrogate for an unavailable ocean) was a proper ritual to assuage Emma's childhood grief. Many backyards are replete with ceremonial graves of Henry the hamster and Fluffy the cat. Adults who organize these rites of final passage for pets have every good intention of helping their children cope with the loss of a living being they have come to love by recognizing the finality of it all. That seems to be the one incontrovertible truth learned by the youngsters—that death is irreversible. It is not the lesson that is overtly taught by their parents, however, who try to convince the youngsters that they indeed will be with Finny and Henry one day. The kids were not really sure what that means—having silently determined that neither do the adults understand their own comforting words that are so counter to what is actually experienced. More effective are the replacement pets bought conveniently and quickly at the local Woolworth store. Why wait for eternity when a second goldfish can be had right away.

It is one thing to lose and instantly replace a pet with alarming alacrity, but when a neighbor, classmate, or relative dies that raises the bar on both sadness and ignorance. Surely, the boys of Sixth Avenue learned from Sister St. Vincent and the other good nuns who shaped their belief system with the eternal glory of their immortal souls that at death "life is changed, not taken away." As an altar boy, Gussie absorbed enough Latin to recognize that phrase when he served at a funeral mass and the mournful *Dies Irae* was sung or read. There is life after death, they were taught, and there would be an ultimate reunion of loved ones. It was a mystery, to be sure, but one that was told with such regularity and conviction by the adult priests and nuns that any mystery that clouded the belief was driven away by simple habit of familiarity. Repeat something often enough and the very sound of the words are thought to be understood. Factual knowledge is overridden by psychological familiarity of repetitive sounds. It is an important lesson, perhaps, in survival. And of course, it is a lesson passed on by countless number of adult generations. Say something often enough and it is no longer questioned. It becomes true by acquaintance. This benign question begging speaks no ill of the beauty and social support of the funeral ritual. The music, the flowers, the kind words, the sharing of sorrow with all the mourners is as important as any human rite that strengthens our fragile humanity. But it is the accepted *finality* of it all that supports the intuitive human conviction that life is over and never to be experienced again—in spite of the oft-repeated words of kind Sister St. Vincent and the *Dies Irae*, that life is changed not taken away.

It is difficult to say how this lesson of immortality plays out in the younger minds. Certainly, they knew what they were taught, especially the vivid descriptions of the believed and anticipated afterlife. It must be noted that they were more impressed by the negative sanctions that awaited those who lived less exemplary lives than the spiritual rewards of heaven that were seemed to involve no earthly pleasure that the boys could relate to. The promised bliss of heaven weighed less on them than the eternal fires of hell. However, if the stories of perpetual suffering were intended to steer the boys onto the path of righteousness, then it was less than successful. Not that the boys were bad; rather, their decent normal behavior was due more to the influence of their parents or peers rather than scary stories of hell-fire. If they literally believed that "mortal sins" that were unconfessed would doom them forever, they would have been candidates for the psychic ward. They were normal kids who through a combination of intuitive common sense and a healthy love, fear, and respect of their parents, did the right thing—more or less. They would feel a greater guilt over their disappointing school grades that saddened their moms or felt more guilt for doing a sloppy job in weeding the tomato garden that angered their dads than any guilt that put "black marks" on their immortal souls. In all honesty, religious guilt simply did not register with the boys of Sixth Avenue with the same degree of severity as the guilt felt from the everyday, real relations with their parents and peers. If Billy were to drop an easy fly ball in center field—now there was the occasion for sincere feelings of guilt. If Ernie threw the ball over the second baseman's head into center field while trying to throw out an attempted steal of second—he would not touch an after-game milkshake until Reds told him kindly to "forget it, Ern, we'll get them next time." There was an honest, human, earthly existence embodied in these boys that was all good—physically and mentally.

The contrast between an honest and contrived guilt was no better seen than in comparing the guilt they felt over disappointing friends or parents with the guilt they were supposed to feel in confession. Once a month—at least—there was an interruption of Saturday chores or ball games at four in the afternoon when the boys would have to confess their sins, manifest sufficient guilt and remorse, and receive the priest's cleansing words that would absolve them from damnation and once again reinstate their eligibility for heaven's bliss (one could never be assured that there would not be a painful stopover in Purgatory first). Boys would conspire at great lengths to compile a list of "sins" credible enough to convince the priest they were legitimate peccadilloes, but not so serious offenses that would prompt further angry inquiries from Father. Ten Hail Mary's and five Our Fathers as penance were proof that the boys had come up with the perfect list of offenses, hoping that they could pull off the same list next month.

All of this is not to say that the boys were immune from any thoughts or experiences about death and/or the possibility of an after-life. Not at all. Each of them experienced real existential encounters with death—some tragic. Reds suffered the horrible tragedy of losing a younger sibling—his six-year-old brother who was playing next to his home when a heavy window box dislodged from the outer wall and crushed the little boy. Big Joe's next-door neighbor—a handsome young man who proudly went off to fight in World War II—was killed on Anzio Beach. Joe was devastated. A little neighbor boy of Gussie tragically drowned in his grandfather's rain barrel while trying to retrieve a toy. Gussie served as a pallbearer for the boy's tiny casket. Billy remembered a somber Wednesday evening after the family supper when his mom and dad were dressed in their Sunday best on a Wednesday! They were talking about their neighbor in the past tense—a kindly woman for whom Billy ran errands. They were discussing whether Billy should accompany them to the wake. Billy was very young at that time, but smart enough to know that the neighbor was dead and that his parents were going to pay their respects. They were wondering if Billy was old enough to go to the viewing. Was he old enough to see a dead person? Billy put together everything that was said and remembers the calm, matter-of-fact demeanor of his parents. They were doing what any good neighbors do— paying their respects to a deceased friend. Their attitude was as normal as if they were going to the movies or shopping or visiting a relative at Christmas. In other words, they were teaching a lesson to Bill—without even knowing it—that death was a natural part of life. There was no talk of an eternal reward or an everlasting hell. There was simply a sad but kind remembrance of a good woman who lived a good full life and died in the company of her family. Billy went along with his parents and had a more honest view of living and dying because of that memorable event.

Socrates of ancient Athens told his jury that sentenced him to die that he did not know what was on the other side of life. But he rationally reckoned that it might not be all that bad. It is either a slipping into a dreamless peaceful sleep forever or a continued state of consciousness. In either case, he was not afraid. He told his condemners that living an immoral life—being a bad person—was way worse than dying. Death as the natural cessation of life is not in our control; living the life of a morally good person *is* something we can control, however. Socrates was not sure about life after death, but he had a practical sense of what living a good life entailed. The boys, had they known Socrates, would have agreed.

Chapter Thirteen

Billy's Notebook Part III:
Antigone Redux

In 1999, Dr. Jack Kevorkian, the late advocate of "the right to die," was convicted by a Michigan court of second-degree murder for ending the life of an ALS patient with a lethal injection. The patient, Thomas Youk, had sought Kevorkian's aid in ending his life and signed a consent form. Kevorkian videotaped the procedure and sent a copy to CBS's 60 Minutes. *He expected to be arrested and hoped for an acquittal that would be the start of the legal acceptance of euthanasia.*

Well, over two thousand years ago, the great tragedian Sophocles presented a moral-legal dilemma that continues to haunt individual human beings and the societies in which they live. In his play *Antigone*, Sophocles depicts the inevitable and interminable clash between the personal moral convictions of individuals and the legal codes of society at large. At the base of every disputed issue over rights and duties is the ultimate question: "Where does one's individual rights leave off and the rights of society's common good begin?" The abortion controversy pits the right of individuals over their reproductive bodies against the duty of the state to protect life. Capital punishment opponents claim cruel individual punishment over against the right of the state to apply the ultimate sanction. Pacifism argues the right of individuals *not* to bear arms in war versus the right of the state to select a military for the national defense.

In the forefront of the news today is the debate over euthanasia. Jack Kevorkian, who has assisted 130 people in taking their lives, injected a lethal dose of chemicals into a Michigan man. The mercy killing—or murder, depending on one's valued view—was videotaped and broadcast on national television. Kevorkian has been tried and convicted of second-degree murder and sentenced to ten to twenty-five years in prison.

It is this latest chilling chapter of the euthanasia debate that conjures up the specter of Sophocles' *Antigone*. The clash between personal convictions and state laws is revisited with alarming endurance.

Antigone is hauled before the head of state, the Tyrant, Creon. She had defied the clearly stated law that enemies of the state who had been slain in battle will not be buried. They shall not be dignified with the soothing cover of earth that will protect their bodies from the ravaging scavengers that would deny them rest in the other life. Antigone's brother was considered such an enemy, and yet she followed the law of her heart, heeded her conscience, and covered her beloved brother with earth. Her love and her duty to her brother superseded whatever the state law had commanded. The law, however, that Creon upholds protects society and deters would-be traitors and enemies from bringing harm to the general populace.

Creon addresses Antigone: "You—tell me not at length but in a word. You knew the order not to do this thing?"

Antigone answers, "I knew, of course I knew, the word was plain."

"And still you dare to overstep these laws?"

Kevorkian knew the law and invited the courts to rule on his act of taking the life of Thomas Youk, a fifty-two-year-old man dying a cruel death of ALS. Like Antigone, Kevorkian followed his conscience and responded to the wishes of Youk and his family to end his life while there was a semblance of dignity. Like Antigone, Kevorkian stood before a representative of the state. Circuit Court Judge Jessica Cooper rebuked Kevorkian in no uncertain terms, reminding him that we are a nation of laws and that his action was a lawless deed that shows "disrespect for a society that exists and flourishes because of the strength of the legal system. No one, sir, is above the law, no one."

Creon and Cooper had to do what they did. Uphold the rule of law. Antigone and Kevorkian did what they had to do. Follow their individual consciences. Greek tragedies die hard. Especially when questions of right and wrong are muddled in a maze of the human condition that mixes individual and social goods. How could Antigone be a lawbreaker? She was burying her brother. How can Kevorkian be a murderer? He was responding with compassion to a plea for release from a life of hell. And who can fault the upholders of law and order who must decide—not for individuals, but for a commonweal? Of course, it mattered not to Antigone nor to Kevorkian what the lawmakers decide. They each acted from sources other than the rational structures of law. They responded to the personal reaches of the heart—the heart that Pascal said "has its reasons which reason does not know."

Antigone is sentenced by Creon to her prison-cave, where she ends her own life by hanging herself with her veil. Kevorkian is sentenced to his prison cell, where he purports to starve himself to death.

Will there be an epilogue to the Kevorkian story similar to that of Antigone? In the Sophoclean tragedy, the blind prophet Tiresias warns Creon that the state has carried out a miscarriage of justice. Creon has confused the "upper and lower worlds." He has failed to bury the dead brother and entombed the living Antigone. This mistake bodes ill for both individuals and society. Creon relents and rushes to give the dead brother a proper burial and to release Antigone from the cave. But as the chorus laments, "You have learned justice, but it comes too late." Antigone has taken her life.

Will blindfolded lady Justice reveal the same message to Judge Cooper? She would have Thomas Youk alive—against his will—condemned to an agonizing "natural" death. She sentences seventy-year-old Kevorkian to a long term in prison that well may prove to be his tomb. Has Judge Cooper confused the "upper and lower" worlds? In her admonishment, she tells Kevorkian that the trial has nothing to do with euthanasia. This issue will be debated with reason and calmer voices long after the memory of the trial and the name of Kevorkian are forgotten.

Perhaps. But if it is the case, that the severity of her sentence is out of proportion to the deed and if the ensuing imprisonment culminates in Kevorkian's self-inflicted death, then the memory of Kevorkian will resonate with that of Antigone. He will be remembered as one who wished to respond to the passionate pleas of individual people who wanted to exercise their personal right to live their final hours with a dignity of their choosing.

"Harry S. Truman celebrates his presidential victory."

Chapter Fourteen

Give 'Em Hell, Harry: Political Science 101

The year was 1948, a presidential election year that saw the popular New York governor Thomas E. Dewey running against a decidedly underdog ex-haberdasher from Missouri named Harry S. Truman. Dewey was the overwhelming favorite with his tall good looks, well-coifed hair, permanently plastered on smile, and his well-connected links to the eastern established republican power brokers. Truman, on the other hand, a short, frumpy Midwesterner with clothes that always looked like they belonged to someone else, would have remained in political obscurity if not for the fact that fate plucked him from the limbo land of vice presidency when the longest-sitting president in history died in 1945.

Wouldn't you know that the very same year, 1948, our boys of baseball were in Mr. Arthur Driedger's public high school's civics class. Art Driedger was a teacher's teacher—young, unassuming, dedicated to a fault, and passionately in love with his subject—the political democracy of the United States of America. He was Tom Sawyer and Huck Finn rolled into one person with an education from a state teacher's college. He was the kind of teacher the boys could respect without fearing him. He could attempt working corny jokes into his lessons without losing control of his class. The students laughed at his humor more in sympathy with him than in the funny incongruity of the punch line. His attempt to breathe life into the lessons with an "aw shucks" demeanor was an endearing quality that his students knew was sincere. The youngsters knew when a teacher was faking it. They could see through poor attempts at humor, angry threats that would never be carried out, peevish language that would have failed Mr. Ryba's standard of self-respect. The boys knew. Mr. Driedger was for real. They knew that the young teacher had recently married and was in the process of building his own humble home. They saw his calloused hands from the manual labor he engaged in when not teaching. They noticed that his dress shirts were often frayed at the cuffs and collars, that his apparently one and only dress suit was getting a bit thread bare. One class day, the students presented him with a brand-new sparkling white dress shirt—size extra-large. They had taken up a collection of their own hard-earned money from doing odd jobs after school: delivering newspapers, going to the store for the neighbors, raking leaves. Many of these public schoolers in his class were emerging from borderline poor to being lower-middle class. They belonged to families that embodied the conflicting fates of hard work, luck, self-reliance, and social safety nets. This was, after all, 1948—the Great Depression was slowly yielding to postwar industrial success. America was at the threshold of becoming a world power, and the destiny of every citizen hinged on this newfound political and economic power.

The presidential election of 1948 was no small matter. Would the social policies of Franklin Delano Roosevelt be continued by this feisty little Missourian who would have never made the history books had FDR lived to complete his fourth term as president? Or, would the conservative opponents of Roosevelt's dastardly and socialistic "New Deal" regain the office and restore free enterprise sanity to America?

On the very day that the civics class proudly presented the brand-new shirt to a deeply touched Arthur Driedger, he announced his lesson plan calling for a mock election, in class, between Thomas E. Dewey and Harry S. Truman. The class would select one student to be Dewey and one to be Truman. Students and representatives would research the issues, Mr. Driedger would apprise them of all the political and constitutional knowledge of the executive branch of government they needed to know, and there would be a debate between the candidates. Finally, the class would vote.

Sometimes it is very strange how certain events turn. Some people believe in fate. Some call it destiny. Others think that things happen because they happen—no special reason other than chance. Whatever! The class picked Billy, our centerfielder of the Sixth Avenue Wildcats to be Harry S. Truman. Billy, the son of a blue-collar immigrant, steel worker, and welder, who barely survived the depths of the Great Depression, a naturalized citizen who had struggled to learn a trade and work his way up from a laborer to a skilled job that would eventually afford him enough money, late in life, to buy his own modest home. Billy's dad would never have made it out of the grinding laboring class if it were not for the social policies of the New Deal. In the grip of the Depression, America was the only industrial nation with no social safety nets for its workers. There could be no collective bargaining of workers and corporations since labor unions were outlawed. The National Labor Relations Act of 1935 was a giant social step to greater economic and political equity for America's working class. One of Billy's prized possessions was a group picture of a local union meeting with Billy's dad standing next to Walter Reuther, the founder of the United Auto and Aircraft Workers. Reuther came up from the mountains of West Virginia to the great industrial north and out-thought and out-moralized the titans of industry. He read the Papal Encyclicals on social justice and the unequal gap between rich and poor. He bargained for profit-sharing between the owners and the workers who produced the products of wealth; he argued persuasively for the moral right of a worker to a living wage. He fought for job security and safety for those who directly put their labor on the assembly line. And he was so successful that the president of General Motors called him, "the most dangerous man in Detroit." And there he was, standing right next to a smiling Billy's dad.

Billy took his role of Harry S. Truman in the 1948 classroom presidential election very seriously. He studied the issues. He read about the New Deal. He knew from his limited experiences how his family's fortunes had changed for the better as a result of the federal policies of FDR—and now, of Harry Truman—if he is re-elected. Arthur Driedger took the mock election seriously as well. That was why he was a good teacher. He knew that his students were learning life lessons of paramount importance. He knew that American democracy was a process, a means to an end, not a completed end in itself, and as such, it was no better than the next generation that had to sign on to this democracy and carry it forth. The classroom of antsy youngsters in front of him was that next generation. He knew they were the future—these future citizens who were thoughtful enough to recognize his need for a new shirt

Billy's opponent in the 1948 presidential election was a classmate by the name of Kenneth (Chip) Evans. A Hollywood casting director could not have made a better call. If Billy was the living example of those political and economic values of Truman, then, Chip Evans embodied those opposite values of Thomas Dewey. Chip was the son of a rather well-off family who lived in a large single home in the upper end of town. Where one lived in town was a true geographic marker of one's status in life. The lower end of town was marked by the Schuylkill River—that same river where the Redcoats were engaged in the centennial celebration. Row homes dotted the landscape of the lower end and gradually gave way to larger homes and mansions of the upper side. The farther one got from river, the more one experienced a better standard of living. The owners of the steel mills, the tire factories, the boiler plants lived in mansions on the upper end of town. The blue-collar workers who toiled in the mills and factories lived in row homes on the bottom. It was a geographic lesson in class divisions—not a generally accepted term in a land of democratic equality—but nevertheless, true.

"Class divisions," "gap between rich and poor," "economic inequality," all of these terms are anathema to those empowered by "privilege." Even this later term is not acceptable in polite cocktail circles. Perhaps these unmentionable terms carry over from the early Puritan or Calvinistic influence. How can there be any other "privilege" than hard work and industrious ambition? How can there be social and economic inequality when every American has the "free will" to make it by dint of his own labor? Any proper Puritan knows that a sure sign of laziness and even ungodliness is being poor. Surely, poverty is a punishment from God.

Mansions such as this were common on the upper side of town. The owner of the tire company lived in this impressive home which later became the Borough Hall. Courtesy of Jack & Brian Coll

In spite of the romanticized stories of Horatio Alger, the immigrants of Ireland and Europe that washed onto the shores of this country were hard put to establish any foothold of decent living when they only had their raw labor to offer the economic free enterprise system. It would take, perhaps, several generations of struggle against the power and bias of the privileged classes—and an eventual social acceptance through intermarriage before most of the children of lower class immigrants could "make it in America." That is why, so many of the fathers of kids like the Sixth Avenue Wildcats hoped to see their sons become professional baseball players. It was more than the money—because the early ball players were not paid that much— more than a laborer in the steel mill where Billy's father worked, however. Social acceptance and respectability were the main reasons. When an unknown Italian kid named Joe DiMaggio first exploded onto the baseball world with the New York Yankees in 1936, a writer for the popular weekly magazine, *Life*, wrote, "Although he learned Italian first, Joe, now twenty-four, speaks English without an accent and is otherwise well adapted to most US mores. Instead of olive oil or smelly bear grease, he keeps his hair slick with water. He never reeks of garlic and prefers chicken chow mein to spaghetti." No wonder Billy's father forbade him to learn Italian and took great pride himself in learning to speak English without the trace of an accent. In this way, he paid part of the price of becoming a good American.

Chip was not of the laboring class, but rather third generation heir to a family of store owners. Chip's house was cleaned and his clothes washed and ironed by a "colored" woman who lived on the lower end near the river. One of Chip's duties was to pick up Mrs. Graham once a week so she could put his house in order. And he was chosen (by fate?) to represent the political and economic values of Thomas E. Dewey in the 1948 presidential elections. As it was said, events take strange turns.

Chip wasn't a bad person—although some of his values seemed strange to some of the Wildcat ballplayers who got to know him in high school and were surprised when he wanted to participate in some of their social activities. He had his own car, for example, and would always collect money for gas from the other boys when it was his turn to drive to the social centers. On a class trip that required an overnight at a hotel, he would stuff his suitcase with towels and robes from the hotel—although he had no need for these items. At a restaurant, he left a tip for the waitress under a half-filled glass of water, which he adroitly turned upside down enclosing the coins. He laughed with glee at the sight of the hapless girl retrieving her money and a dousing at the same time. Even more cruel was his nominating of a shy girl to be a candidate in the ideal high school co-ed contest. He slyly campaigned for her behind the scenes, telling enough like-minded students what a great joke it would be to have this "undesirable girl" win the contest. Chip was sufficiently popular and influential to get this shy, retiring girl elected—and a little embarrassed.

This was Billy Truman's opponent in the 1948 presidential election—Chip Dewey. It was more than just an election over political and economic differences. For Billy, this was more of a contest of worth, dignity, and self-respect. Chip was very popular throughout the school. He had many friends and perks to accompany his friendship. Billy prepared for the one debate that would decide the election as if it were the World Series and he was playing center field for the Philadelphia Phillies. The students in Mr. Driedger's civic class read the newspaper as part of the class preparation for the election. They knew that Thomas E. Dewey was an overwhelming favorite to be the next president of the United States. Every poll anticipated the same results—a resounding victory for the New York governor. That was the general air in the classroom on the day of the debate/election that was similar to the national feeling. Dewey couldn't miss.

Chip spoke first as the Dewey surrogate and pretty much laughed his way through the talk. Chip was a bright-enough student, but he had not really prepared as well as he should. He had actually worked harder getting that poor girl elected to a position she had not sought than he did for the important lesson that Mr. Driedger was trying to impart to his students—that elections matter. They have long-lasting consequences. That whoever is elected as president has a solemn obligation to serve all the people of the nation as we strive to forge a common good for all. Chip had erroneously thought that it was more important to embarrass one of his classmates with the phony coed election than to prepare for what Mr. Driedger and Billy took very seriously.

Billy spoke with elegant, prepared passion of the values in continuing the social policies of the New Deal. He warned of returning to a laissez faire economy that rode rough shod over the very labor that produced the wealth—America's working force. He spoke of the vagaries of a sometimes-cruel business cycle (that he learned of in Mr. Towne's economic course) that, if free from any restraints, punished millions of innocent people. He spoke of the melding of common sense and common decency whereby ordinary folks like the parents of the students before him would be able to afford a decent standard of living. He warned of a return to the rugged Individualism of the era of Robber Barons (that he learned of in Mrs. Crossmore's history class) in which workers were treated as mere replaceable parts of the very machines they operated. Most of all, he spoke of the ideals of democratic fair play and the promise of equality of every citizen. There could be no fulfillment of equality under the law if the economic power and privilege of the few denied the political equality of the many.

Near the end of his speech, Big Joe, Billy's friend, neighbor, and Wildcat teammate, arose from his seat in the back row of the class, towered over the students with his six-foot adolescent frame, and bellowed, "Give 'em hell, Harry!" The class erupted in shouts and applause. The ballots were counted. The election was over. In what was said to be the greatest upset in the history of America's presidential elections, Harry S. Truman defeated Thomas E. Dewey, sixteen votes to twelve. At his side desk, decked out in a new brilliantly white dress shirt, Mr. Arthur Driedger was beaming with delight.

Billy's father (front –center) was a charter member of the local UAW where he worked. He stands to the right of Walter Reuther, founder of the United Auto and Aircraft Workers.

Chapter Fifteen

Billy's Notebook Part IV: Shaping a Democratic Personality

*B*illy had apparently read a book by the American philosopher John Dewey (no relation to Thomas E.) and had prepared an essay on what it meant to develop a democratic personality, implying that democracy is much more than a mechanical system of governing, that it entailed a certain way of life that shaped a certain type of personality. His seemingly unfinished article appears to have been written shortly after September 11, 2001, and criticizes the decision to invade Iraq rather than rectify a bad situation in Afghanistan.

The famous and influential American philosopher John Dewey addressed the National Education Association in 1937 and delivered an insightful message on the value of living in a social democracy. Dewey was not naïve in his appraisal of democracy. He knew it made great demands on people. It requires a lot of faith in human nature, faith in human reason and pooled cooperation. There could not be police on every corner in a democracy. There has to be trust and a willingness to hear views that disagreed with your own. Many times a democratic way of life demands that individual self-interest be curbed for a greater good. Basic principles of fairness have to be upheld. One cannot claim rights that are not granted to others. Justice has to be implemented through reasoned dialogue and debate. Discriminatory and repressive actions must be eradicated de jure if not de facto, and there is a limit to how much injustice any society can endure before it topples under its own oppressive weight of intolerance.

These democratic qualities that Dewey so carefully detailed are embodied in what he called "a democratic personality." By this, Dewey means that Democracy is more than simply the mechanics of a political system to be learned by students in Political Science 101. It is that of course—a tripartite system of checks and balances, but when Dewey speaks of a democratic process that develops a unique social and political personality, he is identifying democracy with a way of life. And it takes a special kind of political personality to make a democracy work. There is a tendency on the part of people accustomed to a democratic way of life to take all of this for granted. Dewey did not. He knew that democracy had to be shaped anew by each successive generation. There is no guarantee that a democratic life will prevail from generation to generation. This is why education was important for democracy's success since education plays a vital role in shaping the qualities of a democratic personality. For Dewey, democratic education called forth the human desires for autonomy, freedom of choice, security, order, and the important qualities of justice and fair play.

Education, as Dewey clearly knew, was not the sole responsibility of formal schooling. All of the social institutions included under the umbrella of political democracy play a vital role in shaping a democratic personality. Dewey explicitly mentions families, corporations, churches in addition to schools. None of these institutions within our democracy is a democracy *per se*, and Dewey wisely notes that, even so, they must not be arbitrary and dictatorial in their assertion of power and authority. A political democracy will be weakened to the extent that arbitrary power is wielded in families, businesses, churches, and schools.

A child raised in a family in which blind obedience is demanded at all times and at all stages of a child's life, a child reared in an atmosphere that makes no appeal to reason and no appeal to anything but threats and fear will produce an unquestioning adult blindly following a political authority with the same timidity expected in the family. The same results will follow arbitrary and capricious authority in the businesses, churches, and schools. Democracy is severely weakened and threatened by such nonrational responses to authority. The ability of citizens to engage in the required critical thinking necessary for democracy simply will not happen if families, schools, corporations, and churches stifle all independence of thought and require nothing but fear-induced obedience. Dewey's precise words were: *After democratic political institutions were nominally established, beliefs and ways of looking at life and of acting that originated when men and women were externally controlled and subjected to arbitrary power, persisted in the family, the church, business and school, and experience shows that as long as they persist there, political democracy is not secure.*

Dewey fears that a nation will be a democracy in "name only," if its people are not imbued with an abiding sense of both free individual expression and a common cause. The very essence of a democratic personality demands this fair play in resolving disputes through dialog and debate as opposed to armed conflict.

The political lesson taught by John Dewey has significant applications today—especially in regard to the grave crisis we face in Iraq. Taking a lead from Dewey, the question is posed: Do the people of Iraq have any chance of acquiring a collective democratic personality?" If Dewey's assumptions are correct, then it is clear that the imposition of a democratic structure—the mechanics of a democracy—will not assure that the people will manifest a democratic response. It would seem that a specific culture of a people with a democratic personality will implement the mechanics of a democratic government, not the other way around. One can hardly assume that the simple removal of a dictator who embodied the practice of "arbitrary practice" that set Sunni neighbor against Shia neighbor will result in anything more than a "democracy" in name only.

The case in our own democracy clearly indicates that it was the founding fathers who conceived the democracy because of their way of life. The Englishmen that established our democratic rules of governance in Philadelphia in the eighteenth century certainly had democratic personalities. They were educated men steeped in the tradition of fair play and the rule of law. The Magna Carta with its appeal to rights and shared authority loomed large in their history. Every attempt was made at rational appeals for fair treatment before rebelling against palpable injustices that were embodied in the Divine Right of the King who arbitrarily ruled over them. Self-rule was what their democratic personalities envisioned and if they were aware of their own intolerant hypocrisy—slave owners for some—at least they laid out a government that is an open-ended process with built in corrective remedies for injustices.

The point is that the founders of our democracy were already possessed of a culture that enabled them to establish democratic structure of our familiar government. That culture created the democracy, and it is difficult to imagine how the superimposition of a democratic structure on a people with little or no formulation of a democratic personality will be a successful venture.

"American philosopher, John Dewey, wrote eloquently about American Democracy as a way of life."

Chapter Sixteen

Ernie's Hiking Trip

The Sixth Avenue Wildcats were pretty good at the all-American game of baseball—the national pastime—but were not really into hiking or camping or joining nature groups like the Boy Scouts of America, which seemed to be at its popular zenith during their teen years. The Boy Scouts organization seemed at that time to be intertwined with local Protestant churches, which were well suited to promote the clean-cut image of America's youth, faithful to God and Country—in that order. "Fellowship" was the operative term espoused by the churches then, specifically, Christian fellowship that went hand in hand with "fair play" and citizenship. The churches were eager to show that being a good Christian and being a good citizen were synonymous. A future professional career in a white-collar job, after attending college, of course, were unwritten goals of scouting, which subtly combined the values of economics, politics, and good old Protestant work ethics.

It was no accident that all five scouting troops held their weekly meetings at the local Protestant churches. It simply was not within the radar of the Sixth Avenue gang to become Boy Scouts—neither was it an aspiration to go on to college or become a bank vice president. The blue-collar Wildcats were destined, after high school, to work at the nearby steel mills or tire and rubber plant. It is no coincidence that all the upper-side scouting members of Mr. Driedger's civics class voted for Thomas E. Dewey while the lower-end non-Scouts voted for Truman.

It was very surprising, therefore, when Ernie announced one spring that he had joined a Boy Scout troop that met at the local Methodist church. It would be much later—after the boys were grown, that the three ethnic Catholic churches would sponsor scouting troops and host the meetings of the new all-Catholic troops at their respective parishes. Ernie had been given some sort of informal exemption and joined the group of Methodists in the wholesome American experience of scouting. Mothers of the other team members would have never approved and Ernie's mom was subject to more than one nasty remark about "joining a heretical group." Billy's mom reminded him of a conversation they had about a year ago, when Billy wondered why he never saw Eddie DiDonato in church on Sunday. Eddie never went to catechism classes either. He is a Catholic, isn't he? He's Italian, and all Italians are Catholic. Billy's logic was impeccable. Billy's mom reminded him of that conversation and how she told him that during the Great Depression of a few years ago, the local Baptist church had set up food kitchens for the hundreds of families whose breadwinner was out of work. Most of these unfortunate ones were from the laboring class—Catholics and Italians among them, who would get food in exchange for lessons and liturgies of the Baptist church. Eddie's father had converted to the Baptist faith, and in so doing, the entire family became Baptists. The oxymoronic expression "Italian Baptist" did not roll easily off the tongue. Billy's mom told the story with all the drama of a tragedy in which members of the One, True, Catholic Church were wooed away from their faith and have become apostates living in the damnable state of mortal sin. She was quick to assure Billy that Ernie was not an Apostate, but there was the "occasion of sin" that lurked in the shadows of every scout meeting at that church and that the church was employing the same tactics with the young scouts, tempting them with the fun and games of scouting, as they had by offering food to the poor in exchange for their faith. Billy suspected that his mom played a minor role in bringing scouting to the Catholic churches a few years after their conversation about Ernie.

But here was Ernie in his scouting uniform telling his teammates about all the fun he was having. He was learning great things about camping and hiking—setting up tents, making, and cooking hunter's stew, building proper campfires, rubbing candlewax on the bottom of the mess kits to avoid the pots from turning black from the open fire, tactfully digging waste facilities in the woods when needed (more about this venture later). And what seemed most foreign and hilarious to the incredulous friends of Ernie, he was learning to tie knots—nautical knots. "Why are you tying nautical knots, Ernie?" asked a skeptical Gussie. "You don't even own a boat." A frustrated Ernie explained how the ties would be helpful in camping and setting up tents, but most importantly, he would earn merit badges for his mastery and these symbols would adorn his already-spiffy uniform.

Ernie's goal in showing off his scouting uniform to the boys was to convince them to go on a camping trip. He had it all planned. They would go to the Delaware Gap campsite where part of the Appalachian Trail crossed over from Pennsylvania to New Jersey. He already got permission from his scout master to borrow a couple of tents and the necessary sleeping bags and cooking utensils. All he needed was Reds to get his father's station wagon to haul the boys and supplies up to the campsite. As previously stated, camping was not in the genetic makeup of the boys Ernie was trying to enlist in his effort to earn a few merit badges. They thought he was joking. In fact, they joked about his request. *Really* joked, by making up popular "Swifty" jokes that were the current rage. The Adventures of Tom Swift was familiar to every boy learning to read in the pre-TV era of the Wildcats. The "swifty" jokes were puns that used adverb modifiers that related to the main idea. The boys aimed the barbs of their Swifty puns at Ernie's proposed camping trip.

"Right, Ernie," Gussie said. "'Let's build a campfire,' Tom said *warmly*."

Big Joe's Swifty: "'That Mountain is not *too* high to climb,' Tom said *haughtily*."

Billy's Swifty: "'We can roast some corn,' Tom said *huskily*."

Reds' Swifty: "'Can we swim in our underwear?' Tom asked *briefly*."

And so it went. Silly Swifty's that set them goofy with kid laughter. Even Ernie who was a bit hurt at their mocking jokes laughed as well, and even contributed a Swifty: "'Cut it out,' Tom said *sharply*."

In the end, much to Ernie's delightful surprise, they agreed to go on a hiking trip. Reds, always the quiet leader, convinced the others that it might not be a bad idea—and it gave him a legitimate excuse to drive his father's car.

On a beautiful weekend in late spring, the boys, with Reds at the wheel, headed up the northeast extension of the Pennsylvania turnpike. Ernie had brought all the provisions as promised. He had two tents, a cooler of food for the hunter's stew that he would cook over an open campfire: cubed beef, potatoes, carrots, onions, and the necessary condiments. He had mess kits for eating and cooking, candlewax to coat the bottom of the pans, plenty of matches, in case he could not start a fire the "Indian way," and canteens for water. They would register at the campsite on the New Jersey side of the Delaware Water Gap, do some hiking, and return to camp for a hearty meal. Things went pretty much as planned. They signed in with the park rangers and selected a site for their tents. Ernie was a bit of a newcomer at tent pitching and had a difficult time getting them set up. Gussie helped him a bit while the others, who, with shrewd foresight, brought along their baseball bats and mitts— just in case—were playing a red-hot game of pepper.

Finally, the tents were up and the boys set out on part of the Appalachian Trail that ascended gradually up a groomed trail leading to Sun Fish Lake at the top. As they neared the lake, they saw a wisp of smoke on the horizon and heard a noisy helicopter shattering the silence of the woods. On reaching the lake, they witnessed the chopper scooping out huge volumes of lake water with an inverted bell-shaped attachment. The helicopter carried the water over the horizon toward the column of smoke. The boys sat at the edge of the lake and watched this unusual fire-fighting technique for about forty-five minutes.

They realized soon enough, however, that they were hungry and wanted to return to camp eager to sample Ernie's merit-badge-winning stew. They had to admit that hiking wasn't so bad after all. They enjoyed the open air and scenery. Some of the views of the gap were spectacular as they hiked back to their campsite.

About halfway back down the trail, Reds and Billy, who were slightly ahead of the rest, came to a sudden halt. About thirty yards ahead of them, lumbering along on the trail and heading straight for them was a big black bear. The bear had its head down and seemed oblivious to its surroundings as it swayed from side to side in its meandering way. "What do we do now?" Billy whispered to Reds as the others came along side. They were in awe of this creature the likes of which they only experienced at the zoo. And here it was in the wild and in the flesh, right before them. "Should we throw a stone at it and chase it away?" asked Gussie in a voice that seemed too loud for the occasion. Just as Reds was saying, "Let's stand real still and see what happens," the bear rose up, sniffed the air, and lumbered off in a different direction. Without a doubt, this was the highlight of their camping trip. They had encountered a real bear. Ernie suggested a name change for their team, from Wildcats to Black Bears, a proposal that was not popularly received.

They were so preoccupied with bear talk that before they knew it, they were back at the campsite and starving for the Boy Scout special dinner. They were ready to eat immediately, but Ernie put them all to work. Potatoes and carrots had to be peeled, beef cubes had to be properly rubbed with garlic, cooking pots had to be vigorously coated with wax to prevent blackening that would violate the "cleanliness is next to Godliness" code. While Ernie set the others on these tasks, he was building the proper Boy Scout fire that would cook the meal. After wasting fifteen unsuccessful minutes of alternating stick-rubbing and flint-striking, Ernie found his matches and lit the fire. After hours of peeling, cleaning, scraping, and dicing, the food was finally dumped into the pot of water and the eager boys watched and waited . . . and waited. It was getting dark and the effect of hunger on the human psyche was taking effect. It is hard to describe hunger pains—especially hunger that afflicts teenage boys. It changes their personality. They were coming close to rebellion when they realized that the meal would never materialize, that Ernie really did not know how to cook this meal. They voiced their mistake in ever agreeing to this stupid idea. They wanted to leave for home immediately. They even questioned Ernie's baseball-playing ability and pondered feeding him to that bear they saw in the woods. Their ravenous hunger had turned to raging anger. When a sample tasting of the stew almost made Ernie himself wretch, the boys' anger reached the boiling point faster than Ernie's pots.

Reds, always the leader who knew what to say and what to do, stepped up to the plate—the dinner plate, as it were. He grabbed his station wagon keys, motioned for Billy to come with him, and announced that he was going into the town and would soon be back with dinner. Hot dogs (already cooked) and milkshakes. Admitting defeat, Ernie slumped toward the tent while the boys, in silent contempt, walked down to the lake and threw stones.

Reds and Billy found a fast-food place not far from the state park and returned in a shorter time than expected with the promised manna of hot dogs and milkshakes—with a bonus treat of french fries that unfortunately had gotten quite cold. When Ernie, seeking redemption, offered to warm the fries on his dying fire, the boys threatened to throw him in the lake.

Night came. Stomachs were full, hunger was sated, enmity toward Ernie fading. Before retiring to their tents, the boys walked down to the edge of the lake. It shimmered in the moonlight, and a soft breeze rustled the leaves in the trees above them. It was quiet and beautiful. Reds told the boys to look up at the sky. With no city lights to pollute the view, the Milky Way embraced them. They could reach up and touch the constellations—our galaxy, our home. The boys looked up in silence until Reds broke the spell.

"This was a good idea, Ernie, thanks."

"Yeah," chimed in Gussie, "Way to go, Ern."

"Good going, Ernie," said Big Joe.

They retired to their tents—Reds, Billy, and Gussie in the bigger one; Ernie and Big Joe in the other. When they had settled in their sleeping bags, Big Joe bellowed out, "There's a bear outside, Tom said *in-tently*."

They all laughed a tired laugh and fell asleep. At approximately 2:00 a.m., Ernie's tent collapsed on him.

Chapter Seventeen

Billy's Notebook Part V: Hiking in Havasu Canyon

*B*illy's notebook entry reveals that he did quite a bit of hiking as an adult. He and his wife hiked the White Mountains of New Hampshire, Bandolier canyon in New Mexico, the Jung Frau Mountain in Switzerland, and many others. This entry tells of his hiking experience at the Havasu Indian Reservation in the Grand Canyon.

The village of Supai in Arizona is a unique village indeed. It is the home of the people of the "blue green water"—the Havasupai whose ancestors inhabited the western area of the Grand Canyon since the twelfth century.

Supai is about forty miles northwest as the eagle flies from Grand Canyon village. For those however without eagle's wings, it must be reached by driving 185 miles from the village to the trail head and then hiking down the canyon wall and over the trail to Supai. It is at the bottom of the Grand Canyon.

My wife and I carefully prepared for our visit to the Havasupai reservation village by stuffing our backpacks with enough food (fruit, granola bars, raisins), bottled water, and light clothing. Early in the morning, we drove south from our lodgings at the Grand Canyon village toward the town of Williams, then west on Interstate 40 and exited at historic Route 66 where we filled the gas tank at the last stop before ninety miles of desert roads to the edge of the canyon. We parked our rented car at Hualapai Hilltop and crawled under our backpacks, ready for the hike down the canyon wall.

Every view of the canyon's 277-mile stretch is said to be exciting, and certainly, we had experienced spectacular sights from the Blue Angel trail, which is one of the favorite viewing spots of tourists who might not favor a rigorous hike. But there was something especially exhilarating about this experience as we stood at the trail head of Havasu ready to descend. The late-morning sun was brilliant as it splashed off the upper jagged rocks and was muted by the smoother, darker walls below.

Our peaceful serenity was broken as a team of pack ponies with its Havasu guide suddenly came scrambling up the last switchback as we quickly stepped aside. The ponies seemed to be racing each other to the top—some of them cutting the trail short as the end of their ascent came into view. Their burdens of fruits and vegetables and milk were packed and waiting at the top of the canyon. Except for an occasional helicopter, these faithful animals are the living life line of Supai village.

The first mile and a half of the trail was steep, rough, and rocky. But the trail graciously widened, and it soon sloped off to a more level walk through the narrowing inner canyon walls. Here, we were shielded from the hot sun and could enjoy the wild spring flowers of Havasu Canyon. The beautiful red Indian Paint Brush was prominent, as were flowering yellow and magenta cacti. At times, the trail followed the stony bed of a washout where we saw signs of a devastating flash flood that wiped out some of the trail and a good deal of crop-ground just a year ago. Estimating that we had covered half of the eight-mile trail, we stopped for lunch at a cool sheltering ledge deep inside the inner walls of the canyon. Our hikers' lunch consisted of an apple, a peach, a box of raisins, and an energy bar. We shared some raisins with a very persistent raven, which was obviously no stranger to those hiking to Supai Village. We drank generously from our water supply at this stop, being certain to replace some of the body fluids lost through perspiring in the dry, deceptive desert heat. We easterners were not accustomed to being hot without perspiring, and the dry air evaporated the sweat from our brow the very moment it was formed. Telltale signs of this instant evaporation came the moment we rested our shoulders by removing our backpacks. The back of our shirts covered by the straps were soaked with sweat.

The rest of the hike to the village was relatively easy, about three miles of flat bottom terrain heavily layered with thick red dust that puffed out from under our boots with every step. A mile and a half from the village, we noticed that the trees were much taller and different from the scraggly pinon pines that dotted the rocky ground on the way down. Soon, we could hear the rush of water and shortly came upon Cataract Creek—a beautiful turquoise clear water from which the native people took their name. Beautiful yellow flowers lined the banks of the cool creek, and little side channels were filled with green watercress that complemented the yellow banks. We crossed a tiny wooden footbridge and walked the last half mile down a hot and dusty tree-lined path to the village. Irrigation ditches catching the precious water ran alongside dry clusters of corn plants. We also saw squash and bean plants and what looked to these nonagronomist eyes like potato plants. Fruit trees grow well in Supai, and the peaches and apricots we saw were quickly ripening. We learned that the villagers were planning to celebrate their annual August peach festival.

The outlying houses on the reservation were low, rough-wood dwellings that imaged the weathered rocks of the canyon. We smiled and exchanged greetings with the Havasu we passed on the road to the village as they worked their crops or rode by on horseback. Visiting campers and hikers are welcome to their canyon-bottom home. In fact, tourism provides a major source of the community's income. We learned that in the 1950s, visitors numbered only in the hundreds in this remote part of the Grand Canyon, far removed from the tourist attractions of the national park. Now, over ten thousand visit each year.

Nevertheless, as we entered the village, we felt a bit like intruders. We were aware of the oppressive treatment meted out to the Havasu. The reservation in the canyon was decreed into existence by the US government in 1880, and the people at that time were limited to only 518 acres of land. Only a few hundreds of those acres could be irrigated for crops. Before the white men came, the Havasu farmed the bottom of the canyon only in the summer, and in the winter, they hunted the top ranges, but by 1900, they had lost to cattlemen and the government 90 percent of their hunting lands on the high plateau above the canyon. They were forced to abandon their native language, dress in the clothing of the white man, and send their children to English-speaking schools at the top of the canyon. Their sad history worked through our brains as we walked the last quarter mile of our almost-four-hour hike down into the canyon and to the rough-hewed timber lodge the natives had built for visiting hikers.

We soon lost any feeling of alienation, however, when we finally ended our odyssey in the center of the village. There were children playing in the school yard, older folks sitting in the front of the general store minding everybody's business, a few tired hikers drinking Cokes on the porch of the village café. It sure wasn't the Grand Place of Brussels, but this hot and dusty village center looked like the friendliest place in the world. Maybe it was the dogs. The village dogs were everywhere— rolling in the dust, playing with the children, chasing after the ponies on their way up the canyon. Supai must have the happiest, dustiest dogs in the world.

We registered at the lodge that was adorned with colorful balloons celebrating the birth of a newborn son of Thomas, the manager of the lodge. The happy new father showed us our sparse room where we would spend the night before ascending from the canyon the next day. Thomas informed us that there was no running water from the spigots in our room due to a short in the village generator. Backpackers in the campground could use their purification tablets, but we of the tender foot tribe staying at the lodge had to preserve the drinking water we carried in. The general store was completely sold out of bottled water and had its potable items reduced to a few quarts of Welch's grape juice. Luckily, we had carried in a good supply of water. Thomas gave us another bit of advice for desert hikers. He reminded us not to forget to hang our hiking boots on the wall hooks before we retired for the night.

We tried to make the most of our short stay at Supai. After a short rest, we hiked about a mile and a half through the canyon to see the beautiful Havasu waterfalls. Havasupai—the land of the blue green waters! In the early evening, we chatted with some school-age children who were eager to know how and why we came to Supai all the way from Pennsylvania. A young Havasu woman working in the café told us that the school year had ended, but there was a summer reading program for those with reading difficulties. Also, there was a GED preparation class that had begun. Unfortunately, she informed us, both programs were cancelled because of the power outage.

We retired to our cabin tired after a strenuous day but extremely satisfied. We wanted to begin our trek out of the canyon at five the next morning in order to get a head start on the difficult sun that we would encounter at the steepest part of the trail. We collapsed on our beds forgetting Thomas's advice to hang our boots on the recommended hooks. Luckily, I decided to shake any loose dirt from my boots before putting them on the next morning. As I turned the boot upside down, out dropped an undersized scorpion, which quickly scurried into a dark corner of the cabin. It was all the prompting we needed to get that early start up and out of the canyon. We resolved to pay close attention in the future to the advice of wise people. It was a lesson we never forgot.

Several days later, we ended our visit at the more-popular Grand Canyon village and took a connecting flight back to Philadelphia from the Las Vegas International Airport. It was an 11:30 p.m. red eye flight. As we roared down the runway and lifted into the night air of Las Vegas, we saw from the plane the gaudy glitter of the Vegas Strip below. Bright, blinking neon towers of red and green and yellow seemed incongruous in the midnight desert. We thought of the enormous amount of energy expended in lighting up that garish playground. Then we thought of the blown generator at Supai village, which left the Havasu without water and cancelled summer school. For us educators, it was a lesson in values clarification.

Chapter Eighteen

Silent Spring?

The Sixth Avenue boys of summer engaged in other teen activities during the hot days of summer. Some of them fished in the polluted waters of the Schuylkill River, which defined the southern boundary of their town. These pre-Environmental Protection Agency days were devoid of any safeguards of fouling the formerly pristine waters that nature had provided for the species of human and animal life. There were too many creations of the industrial revolution conveniently located on that mighty river to prevent fouling the waters with chemicals from steel mills, battery factories, boiler plants, tire and rubber plants. The days of being "stewards of the earth" were a long way off. Earth Day and Rachel Carson were still light-years away as industries competed for both cheap immigrant labor and first prize for polluting both air and water.

The families of the tenacious Wildcats lived across the river from a large cement factory that produced the basic ingredient of every structure built in this small World War II town. Periodically, somewhere between sundown and sunup, the cement plant would release its waste material into the air. The prevailing westerly winds would carry the residue across the river and deposit a thin gray film of cement dust over the entire lower west end of town. Each morning, the working people living in the row homes near the river would awaken to find a strange coating of dust on their rooftops, porches, and windows. The trees that grew in their small yards had their shiny leaves dulled by the grayish powder of cement. Those lucky few who owned cars parked in the street out front would discover that every car had assumed a similar color overnight, as if a magic fairy had decided to bestow a paint job blessing on the car owners. Gray was the fairies' color of choice. Only by the location of the parked car could the luckless owners identify their automobile, since they all looked the same.

Poisonous insecticides were hazardous to birds, animals and human beings. Rachel Carson's book, *Silent Spring* aroused the public to its deadly effects.

Left unwashed, the cement dust would quickly work its chemical magic and soon render the car pitted with a pox-like finish that neither washing nor waxing could forestall. Thus was created a Saturday morning ritual that all car owners on the block performed of necessity. The cars had to be washed and purged of its original sin of cement. Just as with the spiritual baptism of all these good Catholics on Sixth Avenue, in which the baptismal waters washed away the sin but the fallen nature of man was still the cause of future failings so, too, the healing hose waters removed the stain of cement dust each week from their cars, but the original cause remained across the river in the form of the that goddamned cement plant. That was what the folks called the plant. There was Ajax Cement, Portland Cement, and goddamned Cement. When Gussie was in first grade, his teacher, Mrs. Nace, asked all the children to identify their father's place of employment. Gussie innocently spoke the popular name bestowed on the factory by the adults of the neighborhood. It was cursed so frequently that Gussie thought that was the plant's actual name. Gussie's mom was quickly called to account by the stern Mrs. Nace who demanded an explanation of such vulgar behavior from one of her charges.

The industrious Wildcats were soon to create a cottage industry of car washing on Saturday mornings when they would wash a willing neighbor's car for fifty cents (for sixty cents they would provide the soap). Many a bat and ball were purchased from this cleansing source of revenue. Billy could not join his buddies in the car wash business until he first washed his father's car according to the meticulous plan laid out by his father. The hose had to be attached to the water bib in the coal cellar under the house; a rope tied to the other end of the hose was then tossed over the coal bin and out the cellar window, which opened up under the wooden front porch. Billy would then run outside, reach under the porch, and pull the hose through to the curb ready to hose down the cement-covered car. A soft rag applied the soap suds, and after a second hosing, the car was dried with a genuine chamois, which Billy's dad prized so much that Billy thought it was a family heirloom.

Every week, the ritual of washing the car was explained to Billy as if he were being told for the first time. "Son. You have to tie the rope to the hose properly or else you will not be able to pull it under the porch from the cellar."

"Son, you have to have the right mixture of soap and water in the bucket in order to remove the cement dust from the car. Too much soap will streak. Too little won't remove the dirt."

"Son, you have to be sure the chamois is damp enough to remove the soap residue but dry enough to absorb the remaining water."

Every week, Billy patiently listened to his father repeat the very same instructions and patiently nod his head while glancing down the street to see if his buddies were getting ready to play ball. And each week, when Billy was finishing up the ritual and ready to reverse the hose-retrieval procedure, his father, upon close inspection, would discover areas of the car that Billy "missed." Billy often wondered how washing a car could be turned into a super complicated task—and one that apparently could never be completed to an adult's satisfaction. Perhaps his Saturday car-washing experiences explains why Billy, as an adult, took his car to a car wash and never touched a bucket or chamois again.

A more significant reflection of Billy and many of the other boys was why there was more concern over the cement dust on their parents' cars than there was over the cement dust all the people were breathing. One wonders how many of those good neighbors suffered from chronic lung disease. Most of the adult males in the neighborhood exhibited an extraordinary hacking cough that most people attributed to the heavy cigarette smoking of the men. In addition to the daily struggles of trying to pay the monthly rent on their row homes, feed their hungry families, properly clothe their children, these fathers of the second greatest generation were slowly coughing away their lives with a two-pack-a-day habit that was aided and abetted by a daily dusting of deadly cement dust.

Billy and Gussie would often try their luck at fishing in the river on Sunday afternoons after attending the children's mass at St. Anthony. Of course, they would also stay after mass for catechetical instructions from the good sisters of the Society of St. Joseph. Then they were free. The river had a plentiful supply of carp and catfish—not the most delectable of sea food aficionados, but for people living on the edge of poverty and respectability, a meal was a meal.

The boys had homemade hand lines pieced together from an assorted array of string they had collected from old packages, sinkers that were discarded spark plugs rescued from a scrap yard, and floats that were old corks from empty wine bottles. The baited their hooks with "American" white bread that lumped around the hook very nicely. On this particular Sunday afternoon, there was a brilliant sun shining off the river and a warm breeze rippling the water. As they prepared to throw in their lines, several large carp broke the surface of the water about twenty yards from the bank where the boys had settled in. It was a good day for fishing. Billy had the first luck when he caught a sun fish—a small creature whose prism-like scales reflected a tiny rainbow on its side. "Sunnies" were fun to catch and pretty to the eye, but of no other value that would warrant keeping them. Billy tossed the fish back into the river.

The boys noticed two other anglers fishing about a hundred yards away but on the same peninsular part of bank that jutted into the river. This was Billy and Gussie's favorite fishing spot which was difficult to find for any one not familiar with the river. A path along the north side of the water, which was pretty well hidden by trees, disappeared at the very narrow edge of the water where one could nimbly use stepping stones to gain access to a wide piece of land that jutted a quarter of the way into the river. One who was not familiar with the river from up-close would think that there was a tree-covered island in the middle of this wide and fast-moving river. Occupants of cars driving over the bridge into town would make this visual mistake and possibly wonder how on earth those boys got out onto that island to fish. They must have a boat.

The boys were curious about the two men who were unfamiliar to them—in a small town, no less, where everybody pretty much knew everyone. Even more puzzling was their fishing garb. They looked like they walked out of a *Field and Stream* magazine. For starters, they had expensive-looking fly-fishing rods, genuine wicker baskets to hold any fish they might catch, and authentic floppy fishing hats replete with an assortment of fishing flies properly affixed on their hats. The crème de la crème of their attire, however, was the chest-high waders that each of the young men were wearing. They seemed totally misplaced, dressed as they were, at this polluted river running through a gritty industrial town. And as a matter of fact, they were. The young men were from New England, the Green Mountain State of Vermont, to be precise, where their fishing attire would make sense as they waded in the clear streams casting for trout or bass or perch. But here in the murky waters fouled by a variety of chemical pollutants from steel, cement, battery, and boiler plants, they appeared incongruously as an opening to a comic vaudeville routine.

They removed their waders, packed their gear, and retraced their steps back to the stepping stone access to the boys' heretofore "private" fishing spot. They stopped and pleasantly greeted Billy and

Gussie as they passed by. The young men had completed their first college year at the University of Pennsylvania and, rather than return to their home state of Vermont, had rented an apartment in the prestigious main line suburbs of Philadelphia. They had left everything back in Vermont except their love of fishing and the proper paraphernalia. They chatted pleasantly with the boys, asking about the town and of other possible fishing spots. They politely avoided direct eye contact with the boys' homemade fishing gear, although they did acknowledge the carp that Billy had in his water bucket and the two catfish caught by Gussie. The conversation turned on the quality of the river water, which was quite obvious from pungent odor in the air and the obvious sources of the pollution from the factories that lined the banks of the river. The boys pointed out the cement plant on the southern bank of the river, which explained the thin coating on all the vegetation. Before leaving, the college boys emptied their store-bought basket of carp and catfish into Billy's overcrowded bucket. There was no way that the clean stream boys of Vermont would keep their slimy catch from this unfortunate river.

As a matter of fact, Billy and Gussie never kept what they caught. Their mothers would never allow it. The fish from the polluted Schuylkill River not only were not clean, but carp and catfish were not the most delectable table treats for these good people. Billy's father frequently went deep-sea fishing off the coast of New Jersey and caught fish that was part of the family's diet. He fished for the same reasons he hunted—food for the family. It was more than a sport for him. Sometimes in the winter, he would fish for cod and mackerel, which provided many Friday dinners for his family— in those Catholic days of meatless Fridays.

Anytime the boys caught fish in the river, the recipient of their catch was a homeless man known by the singular name of Tutti. The relationship with Tutti began some time ago when the boys were approached by the tattered-looking man as they were about to leave their favorite fishing spot. Tutti apparently frequented this part of the river in order to solicit fish, or any other useful commodity from those departing the river. They gladly gave him their catch and set up a future rendezvous with him whenever they caught fish.

The meeting place with Tutti was about three blocks from where the boys lived. It was Tutti's beat-up old Ford pick-up truck, which served as Tutti's home and means of transportation. When he was not driving, Tutti parked his vehicle on the side of a remote dirt road leading to the abandoned quarry where the boys frequently hiked the overgrown paths and swam in a canal that ran into the river. From all reliable accounts, Tutti actually lived in his truck.

Rumors of Tutti's past life were varied. Some said he was the son of one of the town's scions, the owner of the steel plant. He had rebuffed his father's offer to marry the girl chosen for him and refused to assume his responsibilities as the town's chief steel magnate. When he rejected his father's offers, he was disinherited from all the family wealth and all other connections of rank and privilege. This version of Tutti's past has a corollary that claims there is a stash of money, thousands of dollars, hidden in Tutti's truck. The story suggested he may have absconded with some of the family wealth stolen from his father before leaving, That when Tutti was sleeping in his truck, he was literally "in the lap of luxury," although everything about Tutti's appearance challenged this local myth.

Others say Tutti came to town as a young man working for a circus and got a young local girl in a family way. He married the girl who took the child and left him a year after the baby was born. A third story has it that Tutti took to drink when his wife and two-year-old son were killed in a car crash in which Tutti, who was at the wheel of the car, tried to avoid a deer on a dark road and struck a tree. All of these stories were part of the town folklore and all were without any substantive evidence. Three things only are certain about Tutti with no known surname. He was homeless, he lived in his truck, and he was an alcoholic. He was often seen with some of his similarly disheveled friends walking down the grassy path to the back entrance of the old quarry. They carried a paper bag with a stale loaf of sandwich bread purchased from the corner grocery store and five cans of Sterno canned heat from the hardware store. Sterno cans contained a fuel that campers used to cook their food in the great outdoors. Tutti and his pals used it for other purposes. The bums, as they were named by some locals, would liquefy the jellied alcohol over a fire and filter the contents through the bread. The resultant drippings were caught in tin cups and then imbibed. How the men were not blinded or killed on the spot from this deadly concoction was a big a mystery as was Tutti.

Billy, who often walked his dog through the overgrown part of the old quarry, would come upon the deadly campsite of Tutti and his friends. The ground would be littered with empty Sterno cans scattered around the charred wood and ashes of their fire that lique-fied the contents.

On this day, Billy and Gussie dropped off their catch to a grate-ful Tutti, who came quickly out of his truck to greet the boys before they could peek inside. He gruffly thanked the boys never mention-ing the bigger-than-usual haul of fish, made double by the generosity of the college men. The two boys stayed not a minute more than necessary, went straight home, and never told their parents of these meetings with Tutti. "Any luck fishing today, Billy?"' his dad would ask, indifferent to any answer that Billy might give. "Naw," Billy would always answer. "Too small, we threw them back." But Billy's dad was already into the second page of the sports section.

The river was not the only fishing haunt for the boys. There was a fast-flowing canal that ran through the quarry and eventually ran into the river. Legally, the canal was on the steel mill property, which had purchased the quarry ground to serve as a dumping site for the slag that would be excreted in the process of turning iron into steel. The steel company had laid a railroad track over the canal and rail cars would carry a variety of cargo to and from the mill. The train tracks ran over a small bridge spanning the canal halfway between the river and the steel mill. Two concrete pillars built into the water supported the trestle, and if you were an adventurous teenager, you could drop between the narrow railroad ties onto the concrete base supporting the bridge. There, sitting under the bridge on a foot-and-a-half ledge with legs dangling over the canal, you could drop your fishing line into the murky water and fish in the most original and secret fish-ing spot any boy ever discovered. Occasionally, this was exactly what Reds and some of his teammates did. This furtive site was unknown to all except the boys—and least known by their parents.

This fishing challenge took on a more-heightened sense of adventure when, after the boys had dropped between the ties and onto the concrete support ledges, a train came rumbling by on the tracks about four feet above their heads. Most times the cars were carrying Coke, which was the preferred fuel for the blast furnaces that produced the steel. Coke was made from bituminous coal and had a high carbon content that was perfect for firing the furnaces. Coke also produced highly toxic by-products of ammonia and coal tar, which added another dimension to the pollution the good people of the lower end of town unknowingly endured. Most of the families burned the very same Coke in their coal fired furnaces at home. It was less expensive than the cleaner-burning anthracite coal. One of Billy's chores in the winter months was to empty the ash bin at the bottom of the furnace and sieve the contents in order to salvage any unburned pieces of Coke that might have slipped prematurely through the grate and into the ash bin. After shoveling the ashes from the furnace bottom into a large bucket, Billy would take the contents to the alley behind his house and thoroughly shake the mixture in a homemade sieve, which allowed the genuine ashes to escape through the holes, but captured the unused Coke. Rescuing even a half of a bucket of reusable fuel was an important budget item for Billy's family even at the price of suffering the consequences of working with wind-blown ashes and cinders on cold winter days.

Billy hated his weekly task of sieving the ashes. His eyes smarted from ashes, and the smell and taste of charred Coke seemed to linger for hours as confirmation of the coincident relationship of his olfactory and gustatory faculties. And yet he did not seem to mind the droppings of grease and oil from the train that shook the tracks above his head, which often found their marks on his clothing. His daring ventures fishing under the railroad bridge and suffering the occasional grease droppings on his clothing was no doubt less hazardous than the breathing the cement-dust-infected air and absorbing the toxic by-products from burning Coke.

At a time when no one was saving the earth and its good citizens, and the Environmental Protection Agency was but a gleam in Rachel Carson's eye, pollution was literally, in the eye of the beholder—and also in the lungs of the breather. "It is all relative," as the saying goes, and relative to the proximity of living near the river was the hazard of living in an unhealthy environment. The homes of the poorest citizens were located in the most favorable sites for the industries that generated economic wealth but least desirable for the health and welfare of the people who lived there.

Tutti was found dead in his truck one morning by the local police—and no fortune was found in his truck. As far as the boys of the Sixth Avenue Wildcats, only one avoided working in the mills that employed their fathers. Most of them died well below the life expectancy of their peers. And as far as the natural freebies in life—the air continued to carry the deadly cement, which painted the cars, trees, and lungs of the lower west end of town; the sun was always a hazy orange fighting through the smog of the Coke-fueled steel mill, and after the town fathers approved of spraying the lower end of town with the new miracle insecticide known as DDT—well, the birds would not be singing for long. Not at least in those trees near the river. Rachel Carson's Silent Spring came earlier, rather than later to this neighborhood.

Rachel Carson pioneered environmental protection.

Chapter Nineteen

A Dog Named Oscar

The Wildcat sandlot baseball team had a mascot—sort of. It was not an official mascot. Had the team a real legitimate mascot that reflected the team's name, they would have needed a cage to enclose a real wildcat—the wild animal kind that would never meet league approval. At one game against the Spring Mill team, a blue jay flew into a tree near the third base line, prompting Big Bill Crawford, the Spring Mill first basemen, to yell, "Hey, guys, we brought our mascot." None of the teams ever thought through the juxtapositioning of team names with real mascots. It was rather neat to see a real live mule on the football sidelines of the West Point Cadets as they played against Navy with their Billy Goat cheering them on. Certainly, not much imagination went into these sandlot nicknames that were just imitations of more prestigious teams.

Oscar was an unofficial mascot in virtue of attending every game the Wildcats played. Oscar was Gussie's pet dog and was inseparable from Gussie. If you saw Oscar coming down the street, look for Gussie right behind. If you saw Gussie first, be assured that Oscar was close by. Now, much has been studied and written about the intelligence of animals in general and dogs in particular. Service dogs manifest an amazing level of intelligence. Seeing-eye dogs in the service of their blind masters are quite literally the eyes of their owners—sometimes gauging the difference between life and death. Service dogs that aid the disabled by opening doors, fetching objects beyond the reach of the elderly, barking to announce to their blind masters that someone is at the door. Dogs of the Canine Corp that aid the police, army dogs that search and rescue—all demonstrated exceptional skill in doing their jobs. Firehouse dogs were more than mere figureheads riding on fire trucks in parade. These smart and loyal Dalmatians would dash out of the fire house at the sound of a fire bell and warn all people with their barking to clear the way for the horse-drawn engines that would be charging out of the firehouse. They then ran alongside of the horses, protecting them and keeping them calm as they approached the flames that horses feared. Amazing feats of amazing animals.

Oscar was not a firehouse dog, nor a seeing-eye dog, nor a service dog of any kind. Yet he performed feats that defied belief—and were so routine and ordinary that those who hung around with Gussie took all those feats for granted. Oscar was a nondescript dog that was hard to describe. He wasn't a big dog—weighing only about twenty-five pounds with his fur soaking wet. He had a wiry coat of gray-black color and pointed ears, one of which was bent at the midpoint and the other chewed off at midpoint—the result of one of Oscar's many fights with other dogs. Dog-pound for dog-pound, Oscar was the toughest meanest dog ever. Gussie was probably the only kid in the world who was never bullied or intimidated by other kids. Gussie simply had to utter the simple command, "mouthful, Oscar," and Oscar would tear into action against any aggressor until Gussie called him off. Gussie's teammates may have taken Oscar's role as enforcer for granted, but upon reflection, and in dicey situations that were borderline scary, they were mighty glad that Oscar was there.

Gussie had a younger brother and sister that attended the public elementary school, which was at a farther distance than the high school Gussie attended. Oscar would walk the children to the school every morning, wait until they were safely inside, and then go back home. After school, he met them at the same school door and got them home safely. A stray dog had once approached Gussie's siblings while walking to school. It is not clear what the dog's intentions were, but it was a dog twice the size of Oscar and was aggressive in its movement toward the children. Oscar leapt upon the dog and seized its throat in his small but mighty jaws. The dog ran off bleeding rather badly and was not seen again.

Many times the boys witnessed Oscar's shopping trips to the local grocery. The boys would be at Gussie's house as they gathered for a baseball game. Gussie, however, was asked by his mom to go to the corner store for some ground meat needed for dinner. Gussie would attach a note and the payment book to Oscar's collar, and the dog would go to the store and return with the meat— untouched by no one except the grocer. At about the second inning of the game at the park four blocks away from Gussie's house, Oscar would come bounding to his usual spot in foul territory and watch over the boys for the rest of the game. Gussie knew he would have ground meat for supper. Oscar's mission was accomplished.

In spite of his ferocious temperament, Oscar had a playful side and performed a number of tricks. He walked upright on his back legs at Gussie's request. He would run in a closed circle appearing to chase his own tail with such velocity that he created whirling dust devils in the unpaved streets; he could roll over and "play dead" for as long as Gussie wanted. He bounced a rather large rubber ball with his nose. Oscar seemed to know how to distinguish the three distinct tasks that Gussie expected of him. He knew when Gussie wanted him to work—taking the kids to school and shopping for groceries, playfully entertaining Gussie and his teammates, fighting for all the honor and glory of dogdom when Gussie was in danger.

At one of the Wildcat's games—Oscar never missed a game— this amazing dog performed another task without any command from Gussie. In the third inning of a game against the Ninth Avenue Cardinals, Big Joe fouled off a fast ball directly back over the catcher. Since the crude sandlot field had no backstop, the ball rolled off into infinity. The teams were able to put several good balls in play (taped balls were used for practice), but generally, baseballs were hard to come by. At the crack of the bat that sent the ball in a reverse direction, Oscar, who sat on the slightly elevated bank on the third base side, leapt from his erect sitting position, ran down the ball, and was back in a flash, tenderly gripping the ball in his mouth. He held it tightly enough to hold on to it, but not so hard as to disfigure the ball. However, it became very clear that he would release the ball to no one other than Gussie. Oscar became a regular member of the team from then on, being designated "steady foul ball retriever." He also was recognized as a bona fide mascot of the Sixth Avenue Wildcats. Much more valuable than an accidental blue jay or cardinal that chanced to perch on a nearby tree.

It is hard to explain, but there was something quasi-mystical about Oscar the dog. Something a bit spooky. It wasn't just his amazing feats that he performed—protecting the siblings to and from school or carrying meat from the grocers—professional animal trainers can claim feats similar and even greater of the animals in their charge. Maybe that is the point that gives Oscar a special aura of the ethereal. He was not professionally trained. Billy asked Gussie one day, "How did you teach Oscar to do all these things that he does?"

"I didn't," Gussie replied, with great candor. "He just did these things. I kinda talk to him and he sorta understands. I never made any great effort to teach him anything. The first time I sent him to the store for ground meat, I was heading for the ball field for our game, when my mom told me to go to the store. I took the money and *the book* and told Oscar to go to the store. It is only a block away and he accompanied me there many times. [Local grocers wrote the cost of food purchased by the immigrant families by writing the amount in *the book*, which was paid off at the end of the month.] My mom was mad at me when I came home after the game, but she did say that Oscar delivered the food to her and Mr. Altopiedi had entered the correct amount in the book which he re-attached with the meat to Oscar's collar." Ever since that first trip to Mr. Altopiedi's corner store, Oscar's shopping trips became a routine occurrence. The neighbors, the grocer, and Gussie's mom were so familiar with these canine jaunts that the unusual has become the expected. Nobody paid attention to it anymore. Neighbors that would to stop in their tracks at the sight of a small dog carrying home lunch meat or pork chops now simply smiled and said, "Good boy, Oscar," and carried on. Oscar, of course, would never think of touching the carefully wrapped food—and God forbid if another dog ever approached

Oscar while on his assigned duty. Even the sight of another canine would elicit closed-jaw snarls from this dog-mystic that would send them yelping away as if they were attacked.

Billy's question of how Gussie taught these things to Oscar could not be answered. He did not overtly train him. "Well, where did he come from? Where did you get him?" Billy persisted one day.

"I don't know where he came from, and I didn't get him from anywhere. He just showed up one day. We fed him and he has been hanging around ever since. We don't know how old he is, but he has been with us for five years now. Mr. Altopiedi told my mom once that Oscar should have shots— especially 'distemper' shots, which we thought was to cure him of his bad temper, but my mom found out that it would prevent Oscar from getting sick. We never got the shots for Oscar because they cost too much money." So there it is. Oscar was not only some sort of canine mystic, but also appears to be immortal.

The lesson lost in these "strange but true" stories of Oscar the dog is one that begs a comparison between how animals relate on an informal level with kids and professional adult animal trainers that invest countless time and money in training animals to perform for the amusement of audiences and monetary gains of the professional trainers. Oscar was never formally trained. Gussie never made a concentrated effort to have Oscar perform. Gussie was not a dog trainer. He was a kid who played baseball and had a pet dog that adopted him. And yet no one can deny that this small dog, Oscar, performed feats that could rival or exceed any dog trick performed in a circus or any other professional venue after years of careful training and handling. There must be something about the spontaneity of youth that exudes fun and success. Just as the boys had fun playing the game of baseball—and would never have had the same kind of fun had they been good enough to become professional players—so too they had scads of fun with Oscar that no professional trainer would ever experience. Oscar was not performing before audiences; neither were the boys playing ball to entertain fickle fans. Both Oscar and the boys were free from the fixed and rigid canons of adult dog trainers and adult baseball coaches. Both Oscar and the boys were having fun—and somehow there was an unspoken contagion of that fun.

One spring day, when Gussie was helping his mom carry wash out to backyard clothes line, his little brother was playing with a rubber ball on the front sidewalk of their row home. He was playing a game of one-player baseball that Gussie had taught him. The player would throw the ball against the front steps. Most times the ball would hit the flat part of the concrete steps and bounce back to the pitcher who would field the grounder and make an imaginary throw to first, retiring the batter. Sometimes the ball would strike the very point of the step and send a line drive back to the pitcher-center-fielder who registered the unassisted out. It was great fun and proved that baseball could be played anywhere by any number of players even if there was only one.

On this day, Gussie's little brother was having a great game when he threw an extra-hard pitch that perfectly caught the peak of the step, sending the ball over his head and into the street. Thinking only of retrieving the ball, the youngster turned and ran out into the street just as a fast-moving car was approaching the spot of intersection with the ball. Oscar was on the front porch sitting erect and alert as he did when he accompanied Gussie to the Wildcat games. When he saw the ball, the boy, and the car heading for a deadly intersection, he dashed off the porch. Barking furiously, he headed straight for the boy and frightened him enough to make him move quickly across the street and out of danger. Oscar seemed to feign an attack on the boy to make him move so quickly. To do this, Oscar had to ignore the car and come within a few feet of the boy to get him to run safely to the other side of the street. Gussie's brother was safe, but the car struck Oscar, killing him instantly. Oscar, the mystery dog, was not immortal, but some now considered him a martyr.

The front steps of Gussie's row home where he taught his brother to play 'one person baseball' against the concrete steps. His talented dog Oscar often watched over the game and the boy.

Chapter Twenty

Billy's Notebook Part VI: A Regal Dog Named Duke

D uke was my father's dog. He was a handsome English setter with a classic long hair gray-white coat and floppy hound dog ears. My father got him as a pup, and it was love at first sight—on both sides. They simply loved each other. My father was not known for outward signs of emotion—being a typical twentieth century male, his role as *paterfamilias* was clearly and unambiguously defined as bread winner and law giver. His social relations were somewhat shaped by the untimely return to Italy by the only family he ever knew—his mother, father, older brother, and younger sister—leaving him virtually abandoned and on his own at fifteen years of age in a country he barely knew. It was difficult to display any outward signs of emotion—with the exception, perhaps, of anger. The anger outbursts he frequently exhibited were a consequence of his frustration in being the provider and fulfilling the societal expectations of a dad, when he had very little formal education and scant training at a trade. He was eventually encouraged by some very wise blue-collar pals to take lessons in welding that were offered at the mill. He worked hard at it and became a first-class welder and was able to provide for his family. It was a long slog for him, and being separated from his parents and siblings at such an early age meant that he received very few nurturing signs of affection and showed even less endearing signs of love. Except when it came to Duke.

Duke and I grew up together. We were like siblings. I actually came first, and two and a half years later, Duke was given to Dad as pup by a friend who had no room for a dog. We actually had less room, and Mom expressed her dismay at the cost of feeding a dog that would soon grow to a significant dog size. But this was a time when men ruled supreme, so Duke would stay and even earn his keep by honing his natural bird-dog hunting skills and help Dad put food on the table in the form of rabbits and pheasants and quail that were in abundance in the yet-to-be-developed fields nearby. Dad hunted a lot. He had a twelve-gauge over-and-under shot gun that he prized as much as he cared for his fishing gear. Dad was not a hunter and fisherman for sport alone. We ate what he caught— frequently. My mom complained when she had to skin a rabbit or pluck and clean a pheasant, but she too was glad for the fresh food—even when we had to avoid biting down on buckshot pellets that were overlooked in the cleaning and cooking processes. I learned to scale, gut, and filet fish. Flounder were the easiest; mackerel were the worst with their oily and foul-smelling entrails.

Dad's original reason for taking Duke off the hands of a disinterested friend was for the sole reason of killing more edible game that would become food for the table. He never anticipated the strong bond that would form between him and this loyal and good canine friend. In fact, in answer to Mom's complaints of unneeded expenses when Dad arrived with the pup, Dad placated her concerns by predicting that the dog would have a very short stay at the house. He said that the dog would have to earn its keep by proving its hunting worth, and if it did not, well, we know what Pete Esposito did when his *cur* turned out to a terrible hunter—refusing to point and not sweeping the field properly in front of his master and never learning to retrieve the fallen game. Mom closed her ears not to hear of the horrible ending of the story she heard too often about Tony Esposito turning his gun on his own dog because it was too much of a financial liability. It ate more food than it hunted. I have no doubt that Duke would have endured the same fate as the Esposito *cur*, if he had not only become the best hunting dog in town, but what appeared at times to be my father's best friend as well. That is the way it was with those who worked brutally hard for every dollar and had to supplement their food supply with wild animals they hunted down. They had to decide when "pets" were more of a burden than a benefit and resort to drastic solutions. As it turned out, Dad came to love Duke who showed an uncanny reciprocated loyalty to his master.

There are old grainy pictures taken with a box camera of me riding Duke like a pony. Although I was older than Duke, measured in human years, he matured in leaps and bounds past me, measured in doggie years. Here I am, older than the dog, still toddling along and riding him bareback. The picture shows a child in sheer ecstasy holding on to the scruff of the dog's neck, and the dog, standing straight and still, proud and protective of its rider. Sometimes, I had the feeling that Duke was my big brother. He would tolerate with patience and understanding the clumsy handling of an uncoordinated child who grabbed and bumped the dog in every which way that an errant youngster was prone to do.

Stories of Duke's feats were legend in the neighborhood. There was the time when the chicken wire fence that separated our immediate neighbor's backyard from ours was broken. A half-dozen chicks recently hatched from the coop next door strayed through the broken fence into our fenced-off area that served as a kennel for Duke. Our neighbor, Mrs. Ianucci, who so kindly treated the kids on the block to her freshly baked open-hearth bread, was frantic with fear for her chicks when she discovered they had escaped her yard only to be confined in an enclosure for a dog—a large dog. Her shouts attracted half the neighbors who quickly gathered in our backyard right outside of the previously private chambers of Duke. Our family, of course, was witness to the most remarkable event that followed. While Mrs. Ianucci envisioned the worst possible fate for her little peeps—that they would be devoured by the dog, leaving no evidence of their fate other than a few downy feathers, she was shocked with disbelief over what we all witnessed.

Duke, at first, seemed remarkably disinterested in the unexpected guests that visited his lair. He stretched his body as he aroused himself from a warm afternoon nap and yawned. And as the small group of neighbors watched from outside the fence, he quietly moved toward the chicks and nudged them gently with his gallant nose back under the fence and over to their own side. There was no doubt of Duke's intention and purpose. He carefully repeated the motion with all six baby chickens until they were safely home where a grateful and disbelieving Mrs. Ianucci got them in the coop and affixed a board to the bottom of the broken fence. There were many witnesses to this stunning feat of the magnificent Duke who, after an inquisitive and regal glance at his audience of neighbors, casually went back into the shade of his box and resumed his nap.

It was in the late fall season, however, that Duke performed his greatest feats—during hunting season. When the calendar turned up November, Duke seemed to sense the call of the open fields. It was a sight to behold when he knew my father was preparing for the hunt. He whimpered in eager anticipation, ran back and forth in his contained area, occasionally barked softly as he saw my father don his favorite boots and hunting jacket and unwrap his well-oiled shot gun. I had seen my father practicing the hunt many times in our backyard. I was never sure what commands he was giving the dog, but Duke would point whenever he read the signal. He would come to a dead stop, raise his right paw, send his long tail straight back in a perfect parallel line to the ground, and fix his head in the exact same quadrant as his tail, gazing straight ahead in a perfectly frozen point. And this was merely practice.

On this gray and dismal day near the end of the season, my dad and Duke decided to hunt in a neglected cornfield not far from home. It was evident that winter was not far off. The sky was solid gray and a stiff, brisk wind was blowing from the northeast. The entire scene, totally devoid of color, resembled a black-and-white movie. The golden corn stalks were gone, as were the orange pump-kins. There was no golden sunset often depicted in every nimrod's favorite magazine. But what was worst, there seemed to be no game. Dad trudged behind Duke for over an hour. They circled and looped through the pale sickly corn and briar, over the rough stones and holes. Going on the second hour, Duke began looking back over his shoulder at Dad, suggesting that even the animals had abandoned this desolate field. To reach the car, they had to swing through the south end of the field where the ground sloped and ran downhill for about two hundred yards. Even corn had not been planted here, and a few bramble bushes were all that held the fast-eroding soil. About a hundred yards from the car was a huge crater partially filled with milkweed and prickly raspberry bushes. As they approached this hole, Duke suddenly stopped. At first, Dad thought he spotted a rat. There was a small stream running through the crater, and it was common for water rats to inhabit this area. However, when Duke broke into his beautiful point with his head tail and front paw in perfect synchrony, Dad knew differently. Duke never pointed at rats. There was game to be had at the spot where Duke pointed. He broke point now and, dropping low to the ground, began inching toward the edge of the crater. Dad froze in place, clicked the safety off of his shotgun, and patiently waited for Duke to do his work. Everything was still. The sun must have dropped behind the hills about fifteen minutes ago as the sky was turning a darker gray. The only sound was that of a cold wind that rustled through the briars as Duke reached the overgrown crater. He turned his head slightly to see if Dad was ready, and when a hasty acknowledgment was whispered in return, Duke plunged into the hole in a cloud of dust, stones, and milkweed detritus.

It seemed like minutes since he threw himself into the bramble, but Dad knew it was but a few seconds, for shortly out of the dust and noise rose a huge multicolored pheasant. Hovering like a living helicopter, it came straight up, ever so slowly, its great wings beating the air. In that colorless sky, it looked like something from another planet; green, red, brown, all blending together is a surreal panorama. It hovered about twenty-five feet from the ground, when Dad's reaction ended its short flight.

There was no living with Duke on the way home. He stuck his nose out the window as usual, but he was squirming with a special cockiness of a deed well done. At home, Dad tried his usual deception of hiding his accomplishments in the large back pocket of his hunting coat. He did it every time. Holding his empty hands up and claiming that his hunting trip was in vain and there would be no special dinners until his next outing with Duke. The smirking grin on his face belied his weak deception; plus, the open-ended sides of his back pocket revealed the tail feathers of the pheasant he had shot.

Thanks to Dad and especially Duke, there would be pheasant for Thanksgiving dinner.

"The Regal, Duke, never pointed at rats"

Chapter Twenty-One

Girls

It was bound to happen. The inevitable course of nature relentlessly pursuing the continuation of the species. What appears to be a sudden and immediate transformation of physical appearances, interests, desires, movements, tastes, and values is really a slow and gradual change that subtly steals over boys prior to the discovery of girls. The outward signs that herald this predestined event are apparent. The subtle change in voice to a lower pitch frequency with an added embarrassing quake that resembles the sound of gargling with mouth wash, the appearance of a sparse hair growth on the chest—and elsewhere that is not immediately apparent, the awkward movements of here-to-fore agile ball players now acting as clumsy clowns, the explosion of ridiculous facial eruptions that prove embarrassing in close quarters, the even-greater embarrassment of inexplicable lower body changes that seem to take on a life of their own—especially at night while asleep. One would think that God or Nature would have done a better job of continuing the species of baseball players than to have designed such a flawed model as a pubescent boy. Even the term *pubescent* has a crude and vulgar ring to it—as if the one saddled with this label is somehow unclean.

And yet with all the negative connotations attached to this transitory passage from childhood to adulthood, there is a newfound source of pleasure that is as powerful as it is inexplicable. Making matters worse, adults never talk about it. In fact, their very reluctance to engage in any meaningful dialogue about what on earth is happening to kids is a sure signal to the youngsters that it is not good. And there is this confusing rub. How can the strong and irresistible urges that arise with the advancing sexual powers feel so personally good and be so socially bad at the same time? This is the confusion planted in the young by the conspiracy of nature and adults. Nature gives the power of pleasure and adults act as if it is an unmentionable pain.

It is not certain when the Wildcats were afflicted with opposite distraction. Surely, there was no one time when a switch was thrown, and every boy was simultaneously moonstruck. But it did seem that at one particular ball game, similar symptoms were displayed indicating a mass outbreak of attention to something other than the game they were playing. It was in the spring when the team had a home game against the Ninth Avenue Cardinals. Whether or not the Cardinals were precociously advanced in the field of sexual attraction, and may have had a head start on the Wildcats, seems unlikely. Nevertheless, when the visiting team traveled the three blocks from their own neighborhood to engage the Cats in combat, they were accompanied by a bevy of teen friends of the opposite sex. This was something new. The homemade sandlot league rarely had fans in attendance. It was not expected. And now, there they were, four bright-as-buttons teen-friends of the lucky Cardinals. And they were wearing shorts.

All four, talking loudly and not seeming to mind drawing attention to themselves, sat on the grassy elevated bank along third base, their arms hugging their knees as they leaned toward each other sharing secret whispers and glances in the direction of the smitten players on the field. They may have been watching the game, but the Wildcats were watching the girls. A distracted Gussie at third base watched a line drive whiz by him a mere foot away from his belated glove. Had he been paying attention to the batter instead of glancing at the foursome on the bank, he would have snagged that ball. Big Joe claimed he lost a pop foul in the sun, but had there been a ready re-play camera, the real cause of his distraction would have been revealed. There was a surreal aura of giddiness that seemed to overtake the boys. They uncharacteristically giggled at the slightest happening. If they struck out, they giggled. If they got a hit, they giggled. If the made a put out or an error, they giggled with the same degree of silliness. They displayed all the symptoms one would expect of lovestruck teenagers trying to impress the girls with old-fashioned juvenile foreplay. Riding a bicycle in circles with no hands or dunking the girl's pigtails in the inkwell or making silly faces and running away. If the boys were peacocks, their fantails would be in full bloom. It was as ancient and animalistic as a courting dance, the timeless ritual of the male animal preening before his brood and hoping against hope that he would be the peacock the peahens would receive. Sounds silly perhaps; adults might not agree, to be sure. But adults have conveniently lost their memories, now that they have made the major decisions in their lives—they have jobs, are married, and are paying off a mortgage—in that order. Funny how easily adults forget the silliness—and the reality of their youthful courting antics.

On the field, only Reds seemed to retain his sanity. He was a little older and a lot wiser than the others, and he recognized the giddy pre-sexual pantomime that was going on. From his shortstop position, he tried to bring his players' attention back to the game. "Heads up, Billy," he called to his center fielder who was not adjusting his position to the batters as he was accustomed. He seemed more preoccupied with what was happening in the area of third base. "Get in the game, Ernie," Reds implored his catcher who seemed intent on lumbering into the third base foul territory no matter where the foul balls were hit.

Finally, Reds gave up and conceded the game in the fourth inning. The game was lost well before the final out. There was no way he could retrieve his ball team from the four female cardinals perched on the bank behind third base. The Wildcats lost the game badly and giggled off the field—still keeping their eyes, however, glued on the departing Ninth Avenue entourage leaving for home. They did not fail to notice that one of the Red birds coyly glanced back over her shoulder at the boys. If the boys could put words to that glance in the form of a comic book balloon message, they would clearly see the words seductively over her pretty head as "Better luck next time, boys." And they did not think she was referring to the game. Such is the hermeneutics of youth's first love.

Usually, after a game, the team would hustle to Jessie's milkshake shop for a post-game treat. Today was different. They seemed reluctant to leave the scene. They horsed around with a more restless and quixotic energy. They wrestled on the grass, punched arms more vigorously, began making up names for the unknown girls who had visited their sacred baseball lair, and not all of the names were flattering—or printable. The *Swifty* puns emerged with a new flavor of profane male chauvinism. Ernie's Swifty: "Did you cop a feel?" Tom asked *touchingly*. BIG Joe's Swifty: "Does she have on underwear?" Tom asked *pantingly*. Crude? Yes. Demeaning? Without doubt. Excusable? Not really, unless if viewed as some sort of creative and temporary Freudian sublimation necessary to transport the boys safely across the treacherous waters of adolescence.

Gussie then wickedly suggested that maybe it was time to teach Big Joe a lesson for making three errors in the game. He should be "de-pantsed" and maybe have poison ivy dumped on his private parts. The others held him down and actually carried out the first part of their threat, but graciously omitted the ivy decorations, substituting a generous sprinkling of field grass instead. Reds, who participated with equal enthusiasm in this post-game venting, noticed that the sun was beginning to set and recommended that they go home. They skipped the traditional milkshakes this day; rather, they all went to their respective homes—presumably to take cold showers. A new day of discovery had begun.

They would survive the seeming madness of this first encounter with the lurking demi-god, Eros. They were all struck by the arrow of lust. They were responding to all the built-up bodily fluids, psychological drives, and social enticements that leagued against them. They were taken by surprise; ambushed by the internal and external forces of nature and society. The unexpected arrival of the four female Cardinals was merely the occasion of what was bound to happen anyway. The newfound energy and feelings were destined to be recognized sooner or later. Only the overly scrupulous introvert would suppress these feelings and, ultimately, face the consequences of a mental awkwardness much more serious and long lasting than the temporary insanity displayed by the boys at this time. Facing up to the moral quality of what spontaneously felt amoral and good became apparent when they wondered if their words and deeds needed to be confessed on Saturday to Father D'Annunzio. These recent events presented a new challenge to the required monthly visits to the confessional. This was very much a bigger deal than making up how many times you lied to your little brother or disobeyed your mother and father. A wrongly expressed "sin" might arouse the good father from his darkened chamber of mundane venial sins and arouse a host of embarrassing questions that may well be overheard by the nervous line of penitents outside the box. Framing innocuous words around sexual activity so as to slip them by Father D'Annunzio was no mean feat and would take some real collaboration and brainstorming on the part of the boys.

How did they come to the conclusion that the magnitude of guilt over things sexual were so much greater than the petty peccadilloes heretofore confessed? First of all, there was their own felt awareness of the newness, strangeness, and power of whatever it was that surged through them. Secondly, there was no doubt of the social prohibitions leveled against all actions, thoughts, and deeds that even tangently bordered on the sexual. Parents especially seemed to be in league with society in this anti-sex conspiracy. Parents deliberately cloaked sexuality in a shroud of secrecy. There were unspoken taboos as to why certain movies were to be avoided, why some books could not be read, why certain words could never be spoken. Even thoughts that sneaked into your consciousness had to be immediately expunged. They learned this from the good sister St. Vincent, who warned them of "impure thoughts" about a year before they even suspected what the term meant. Now they knew, and it hastened the urgency of a confessional remedy.

Regarding what girls they should associate with—well, there were no overt guidelines given here either. Billy was a senior in high school heading for a movie date with a terrific girl in his Latin class when his father asked him with all embarrassing sincerity, "She's not a pig, is she, son?"

"No, Dad, she's nice." That was the total extent of Billy's sex education from his father. He did not get much more from his high school health and physical education teacher, Mr. Bean, either. There he learned the names of several venereal diseases and the dire consequences that fell on teens if a pregnancy ensued from their "dating." Billy got the lowest mark in his high school career because he misspelled most of the terms in the test—including *chlamydia*, which he originally thought referred to the ancient people of Lydia.

The boys learned more about sex from older students in their high school locker room. Those older guys provided the boys with a wealth of invaluable information—including visual aids. There was an older student known only by the singular name "Link," who always seemed to be in the locker room. There was a suspicion that he lived there. No matter when you entered the boys' locker room, there was Link, gladly revealing to eager listeners the mysteries of creation. Link had a pack of naked lady playing cards. He laid them out one by one, teaching a new anatomical lesson with each card. The Queen of Hearts was the most revealing and informative. Boys would try every reason possible to be excused from class for a quick trip to the locker room to see what card Link was playing. It was an underground education born of necessity to be sure, but subject to searches and seizures by every adult from school teachers and principals to parents and older siblings who seemed to forget where they learned the facts of life. To the best of anyone's knowledge, Link never got caught and his well-worn ladies never confiscated.

The boys of the second greatest generation survived puberty. On reflection, it did not seem as traumatic as first imagined, and they soon learned they could play baseball and enjoy the company of young ladies at the same time, that love of baseball and love of women were cousins born of the same human desire to experience something good. It simply happened that their bodies and minds learned simultaneously how to play and enjoy baseball first while, with sexual desire, the body was way ahead of the mind. It was something like baseball's spring training when the pitchers were always ahead of the hitters. At any rate, what seemed like an eternity of confusion and disarray was more akin to a brief case of the hiccups after swigging down a fizzy cold drink too quickly. They not only survived sexual changes, they turned out to be pretty good husbands and fathers and citizens. They could even look back on their silly behavior and bad attempts at humor (Swifty jokes maybe got an exemption) and wondered how it all happened. If they ever talked about the unsavory "Link," the permanent resident of the boys' room, they did so with a mixture of amusement and embarrassment. As fathers, they would kill their sons if they ever associated with the sleazy Link-of-the Locker Room—or maybe not. Maybe they could transcend their own narrow and socialized values of grownups and understand once again the innocence and honesty of youth—boys of a tender age looking for answers that adults only pretended to know—and would see in their sons a mirror image of themselves going through the inevitable discovery of their manhood. They even learned that the visiting girls from Ninth Avenue were okay. Gussie, in fact, eventually married one of the female Cardinals. Her name was Dolores, and she became a nurse working at a local hospital. They would have a son, wouldn't you know, and when his boy was approaching adolescence, Gussie planned on telling him about spring training and how the pitchers are always ahead of the hitters.

Chapter Twenty-Two

Billy's Notebook Part VII: Poems from Freshman Year

*S**hortly** after graduating high school, Reds and the gang planned a weekend trip at the New Jersey seashore. Gussie and Dolores were engaged to be married, and the plan was for Dolores to drive to the coast and meet up with them after her shift in the hospital ended.*

Dolores drove a tiny Henry J car. It was one of the first attempts on the part of America's auto makers to build a small economy car. Billy described it as an ugly car that had small fin-like fenders that gave the appearance of being a guppy. The Henry J experiment did not last long. The Henry J. Kaiser Company that made the cars apparently were better at building tanks for the army than they were at making reliable automobiles. Not surprising, Dolores and her Henry J never made it to the shore. Her car broke down halfway there and she had to be rescued by the gang. Billy, the only one who went on to college, was home for the summer after completing his first year. Having taken a poetry elective course, he thought qualified to console a disconsolate and carless Dolores. Readers can judge for themselves whether or not it is an improvement over the "Swifties."

For Dolores—with apologies to E. A. Poe

For Dolores

With a car by Henry Kaiser at a price to shock a miser, and a driver, none the wiser, started she for distant shore.

But the brake and clutch and gasket were predestined for a casket—

An unpretentious basket. "Only these and nothing more."

But the coil was beguiling and the carburetor smiling at the tires tired of mileing over roads so rough and sore.

So with nothing else that's spoken, with both car and spirit broken, purchased she, a shiny token. Riding buses evermore.

Chapter Twenty-Three

Billy's Notebook Part VIII: Love, Desire, and Sexuality

Billy apparently attempted more serious forays into the mystery of human desires. His next Notebook entries dealt with love as the strongest of desires, determining what we value most. Romantic love is a denial of death's finality and is the desire for the immortality of heaven; sexual love, on the other hand, is the dark desire of the earth.

The Desire for Goodness

Perhaps no other aspect reveals the puzzling paradoxes of human nature more than the tantalizing feelings of desire that arise from deep within the human psyche. Desirous needs begin at the moment of a human being's existence and grow to full awareness as strongly felt aspirations. No conceptual model seems adequate to explain what is felt to be an emptiness that needs to be filled. Even when desires are satisfied, the fulfillment is limited and ephemeral. We need the stimulating drive of desire to motivate our continued existence, but we are often frustrated by desires that are either thwarted or renewed with greater intensity. Desires are expressed in many ways—all of which indicate the power and limits of human desire: Desire is the *craving* for satisfaction of physical and emotional needs. Desire is the *aspiration* to succeed in a variety of human preoccupations, from leisure activities to professional vocations. Desire is the abiding force of *love—Eros*—which seeks to create through sexual acts of physical reproduction or artistic acts of reproducing the beauty and sublimity of nature. Knowingly or unknowingly, desire is the *yearning* for an elusive happiness that always seems to be at arm's length. Desire is the life-sustaining energy that seeks, but never wholly finds its fulfillment. Desire seems embedded in human nature as a perpetual and paradoxical *itch*, that when scratched, engenders simultaneous feelings of pleasure and pain. It hurts and feels good at the same time.

While desires suggest an internal yearning for some type of fulfillment, there is an external counterpart to inner desires in which something must appear desirable. What is it that evokes desires in human beings? What is it that makes something or some person or some event *desirable*? One could tabulate an endless catalog of qualities based on particular desires of different individuals under different circumstances and at different times. Food is desirable if one is hungry, companionship is desirable for those who are lonely, rest is yearned for by the weary, health is desired by the infirmed. An endless list of desires is matched with that which is suitably desirable. However, the one quality shared by all that is or appears to be desirable is the quality of *goodness*. What is desirable must appear to be good in some way. What is sought after is considered to be of *value* by those who have a desire for it. Much of moral philosophy deals with the discernment of what is *really* good for human beings from a spurious and injurious "goodness."

Desires play a central role in the formulation of moral systems, since it is desire that prompts human actions. Moral value is commonly held to be the ultimate value that determines the very character of human beings. Actions that are the manifestation of a good *person* are valued as basic and primary to human nature. Actions that manifest good electricians or engineers or salespersons, on the other hand, are valued as practical functions of professional life, independent of the moral character of the person. The desire to be a good worker and the desire to be a good person may not always be in synch—even though both avenues are approached by human desires seeking some aspect of goodness. Whatever the case may be—the practical desire to achieve success or the basic desire to be of moral character—the valued notion of goodness is latent in all that is sought by human desires.

Conceptually, an analysis of love may not add any clarification to the puzzle of human desires. Indeed, expectations of definitive understanding may crumble under lived experiences that may cast "the lover" in a more perplexed state of confusion as emotions get mixed and tangled in a net of contradictory feelings. What we thought to be "true love" turns out to be an infatuation, or worse, a cruel illusion. What we had taken to be a superficial relationship grows into a deep and meaningful love bringing comfort and support at life's most difficult times. Does our "love" change as we change? Does the degree and intensity of love depend upon the *object* of our love? How enlightening is it to refer to love's desire as an "*object*?" The puzzle of meaning increases as we expand the range of love-relations. The familial love of parents for their children is in terms of nurture and support. The loving rivalry of siblings within the family unit brings new tensions to understanding what is really felt and desired as brothers and sisters compete for affection. There is the passionate and forceful love of newfound sexuality thought to be the hallmark of adolescence—but perhaps not. Perhaps love as sex is just beneath the surface of human beings throughout their entire existence. Some people seem to love their work—their careers—with all the passion they can muster. Is it genuine? Is it escapist? Who can tell? Patriots love their country and espouse ideals of love for which they seem willing to die. "Give me liberty or give me death." Religious saints and/or zealots demonstrate the same loving fervor for their God. Such intense love has spawned both martyrdom and mayhem—equally for the love of God. We weep as we read of atrocities in faraway places because we love humankind. And of course, we love our pets, our hometown football team, playing golf and butterscotch ice cream. The meaning of love dissolves in an abstract tautology in which we love everything and nothing.

We may not *know* what love "means," but we certainly experience the joys and sorrows associated with our loving or nonloving relationships that permeate our lives. Assuming then that love is a forceful manifestation of human desires that is much more readily experienced than it is defined, we shall attempt three approaches regarding how human beings experience love. First, we shall consider love as expressive of what a person desires most in life. What they hold in highest value is that which they love. Secondly, it will be suggested that the age-old human expression of romantic love is no trivial matter. Romantic love is a very concrete human desire for what each person wants but fears that she or he may not get—immortality. Thirdly, sexuality will be considered as an individual and concrete form of romance disguised as a dark power that has been banished by an ambivalent society which holds sex at a distance—but not too far away.

It is perhaps ironic that while love remains at arm's length from any satisfactory cognitive definition, nevertheless, the strong desires of love that emanate from the depths of the human person highlight and define the very character of the individual person. Love expresses what we desire, what we value. What is more, love expresses an *ultimate* desire—what we value *most*. We experience a gradation of feelings and desires regarding what we esteem as good and desirable. We can thus distinguish having a high regard for someone as compared to loving someone. We can tell the difference between liking something or someone and loving something or someone. Love calls forth our deepest desires. And if we are not aware of the profundity of love's desires, then our values are hidden from ourselves and we live in self-deceit. The term has earned its historical significance. It is not used lightly. Love sums up our character and tells us what is most important to us as an individual person. The summation of love's values gives meaning to life. "Love" and "love of life" are identical, since love is the very embodiment of what we cherish in life. Love, as intimate desire, resides at the core of our existence and is not often revealed in its truest nor fullest form—not even to ourselves. Our ultimate actions betray love's desires and submits our chosen values to the scrutiny of both self and society.

Chapter Twenty-Four

Billy's Notebook Part IX: Romantic Love—The Desire for Immortality

Romantic love carries a commonplace meaning of some abstract and ethereal form of love that is off somewhere in the heavenly clouds so far from human attainment that it never fully impacts on real flesh and blood human beings. It is best left to the poets and songsters to entertain us with fleeting emotional moments of romance that will not have a meaningful effect on our practical daily living. It is thought that romantic love expresses such unrealistic desires that they are relegated to an abstract realm far removed from the practical urgencies of life. Foolish idealism is not infrequently associated with romantic notions of love. Popular meanings of romance aside, however, notions of romantic love have served as inspirations for higher causes and accomplishments throughout human history. And if it seems that such notions as love and beauty and goodness are beyond human expression, it may also be true that if these ideals cease to guide human actions as absolute limits, then we seem to have lost our way as human beings.

The strength of romantic love and its desire for immortality is often attributed to Plato's philosophy—especially as expressed in his dramatic dialogue *The Symposium*. In this brilliant writing, many of Plato's familiar cast of characters are celebrating the literary triumph of the young dramatist, Agathon, who has recently won the prize at the Dionysian festival with his very first tragedy. The exuberant revelers have turned the celebration into a drinking contest. A young physician present at the party fears for their health and suggests a more worthy contest. Each will present a talk on love—EROS—a most important topic very seldom spoken of with any proper elegance. The talks that precede the final words on love spoken by Socrates all contain some obvious and common notions of love. Love is personified as the oldest of the gods, responsible for the perpetual generation of life's cycle. Love serves a useful purpose of encouraging inferior men to do greater deeds. Love is a powerful force that if unguarded could lead to chaotic events. Agathon, the dramatic poetic, delivers a flowery rendition of love as beautiful and fair, sweet and good.

Socrates delivers the final talk, pointing out the partial truths in the previous speeches and offering—as Plato's spokesperson—a philosophy of love that has had a lasting influence on succeeding generations. Love is not anything in itself—not beautiful nor good nor fair—rather, love is the strongest of human desires. Metaphorically speaking, love is born of poverty and wealth, of emptiness and fullness. Through love, we mortals are driven to seek a satisfaction that never seems to satisfy. In this sense, love is a creative principle, driving us to create by the attraction of that which is good and beautiful. The paradox of human nature's ambivalent physical and spiritual inclinations are reflected in the force of love's drive to create that which is material and intellectual. There is a hierarchy of beautiful things toward which we are drawn by love. We are attracted—especially as young adults—by the beautiful form of a person and are urged by love to create our own offspring, our physical children. As we age, we are drawn by love to a wider range of beauty and goodness. We look beyond the physical beauty of individuals and comprehend the beauty of humankind and social institutions. The spiritual "children" of Homer—his literary works—and the spiritual "children of Solon"—his wise laws—are more enduring and good for society than any of their physical children.

Standing behind all of life's attractions that compel love's desires, however, is the ultimate motivation for all that we love—the overriding desire for immortality. It is not simply a question of human love's desire to possess that which is good and beautiful; we want to possess it *forever*. We seek immortality, first through the "love of our life" when we procreate our children; we seek a higher form of immortality through works of art and beneficent societal endeavors that perpetuate the cycle of life. Socrates claims no knowledge for himself; rather, he was taught these truths by a wise priestess, Diotima, who told him, "All men, Socrates, have a procreative impulse, both spiritual and physical, and when they come to maturity, they feel a natural desire to beget children, but they can do so only in beauty and never in ugliness. There is something divine about the whole matter. In procreation and bringing to birth the mortal creature is endowed with a touch of immortality. But the process cannot take place in disharmony. That is why Beauty is the goddess who presides over birth, and serenity and happiness which makes procreation possible. If we as agreed that the aim of love is the perpetual possession of the good, it necessarily follows that it must desire immortality together with the good, and the argument leads us to the inevitable conclusion that that love is love of immortality as well as of the good."

Diotima takes Socrates to a higher desire—a love of immortality through works of the spirit. The greatest love at this level is the desire to create a just and well-ordered society.

Those whose creative instinct is physical have recourse to women and show their love in this way, believing that by begetting children they can secure for themselves an immortal and blessed memory hereafter forever, but there are some whose creative desire is of the soul and who long to beget spiritually, not physically, the progeny that it is the nature of the soul to create and bring to birth. If you ask what that progeny is, it is wisdom and virtue in general; of this all the poets and such craftsmen as have found some new thing may be said to be begetters but far the greatest and fairest branch of wisdom is that which is concerned with due ordering of states and families, whose name is moderation and justice.

Finally, Diotima takes Socrates to the pinnacle of love—the ultimate possession of absolute goodness and beauty. It is the total love of a beauty that never fades, never diminishes, never changes. The beauty that never dies. Knowledge and love of such beauty implies that the lover—mortal though he may be—perhaps possesses a dim view of immortality and perhaps has built up his love of beauty from previous lives. Perhaps he has achieved immortality.

This is the right way of approaching of being initiated into the mysteries of love, to begin with examples of beauty in this world and using them as steps to ascend continually with that absolute beauty as one's aim, from one instance of physical beauty to two and from two to all, then from physical beauty to moral beauty, and from moral beauty to the beauty of knowledge, until from knowledge of various kinds one arrives at the supreme whose sole object is absolute beauty, and knows at last what absolute beauty is. And having brought forth and nurtured true goodness he will have the privilege of being beloved of God and becoming, if ever a man can, immortal himself.

Although Plato intended *The Symposium* to be a triumph of philosophy over poetry—Socrates, the wise philosopher, defeats the narcissistic poet, Agathon. Nevertheless, Plato's own literary style of writing and the mysterious nature of love, beauty, and immortality have all combined to assert a lasting influence on literary creators. As much as Plato would like to offer clear rational arguments for the life-giving powers of human love, beauty, and goodness, he himself seems aware that he is entering quasi-mysterious ground that ordinary language cannot express. This is why perhaps, he has recourse to ironic expression, metaphor, and mythic symbols to announce the truth of love, beauty, and the human quest for immortality. The inner depth of love removes it from rational analysis and ordinary discourse. Language is inept in expressing the depth of love's desires and so love is given over to poetic metaphor. We speak of love overflowing from the heart, or of the love that resides in the soul of the person. Love is depicted as the very wellspring of life, always renewing our desire to be, always defining who we are to ourselves and to others. Whatever Plato's vehicle to express the profundity of an eternal love, he challenges those who would reject his ideals as mere romantic fancy, for without those ideals of an enduring social order based on love of goodness and justice, we cannot live.

In Sonnet 56, Shakespeare captures the Platonic spirit of love as that which is more than mere physical appetite. It is rather the constant renewer of life and the energizing force of relationships. And when it is cold in the winter of our souls, we look to love to restore desire and meaning. Love is our reason for being.

> Sweet love, renew the force, be it not said
> Thy edge should blunter be than appetite,
> Which but today by feeding is allay'd,
> To-morrow sharp'ned in his former might.
> So love be thou: although to-day thou fill
> Thy hungry eyes even till they wink with fullness,
> To-morrow see again, and do not kill
> The spirit of love with a perpetual dullness:
> Let this sad int'rim like the ocean be
> Which parts the shore, where two contracted new
> Come dailey to the banks, that when they see
> Return of love, more blest may be the view;
> As call it winter, which being full of care,
> Makes summer's welcome thrice more wish'd, more rare.

The Romantic Movement of British literature (1798–1832) runs counter to the popular notion of love as an esoteric add-on to life. As Europe was caught in a tumult of political and industrial revolutions, it was the Romantic writers who captured the value of an individual's love of life and nature. They reminded us that life as an individual was worth living. As the Napoleonic wars raged for twenty years—a grim reminder of human frailty and mortality—and, as the burgeoning industrial revolution reduced individuals to factory components, writers such as Wordsworth and Keats located the source of meaning in the individual desire for life. Nature has too much beauty for man to want to leave it. Love is too powerful a source of personal energy to be dissipated by conventional conditions of mass warfare and mass production. Individual self-identity is too transparent and too proud not to want to live forever. We—each one of us—desire immortality. Knowing full well that we are destined to die, we love life and desire to live forever. Love is the source of such desire. This loving desire is not a meaningless abstraction, but rather, the strongest of protests for individuality, creativity, independence. It is also an assertion of nature's beauty and worth—more worthy than what industrialization intends for her.

William Wordsworth's (1770–1850) *Ode: Intimations of Immortality from Recollections of Early Childhood* reflects the spirit of the individual's love of life and nature and immortality. He introduces the Ode with an apology that "nothing was more difficult for me in childhood than to admit the notion of death as a state applicable to my own being." Writing this piece in the beautiful Lake District of England—amidst the natural splendor of ferns and flowers, streams and meadows, sunshine and rainbows—Wordsworth reflects the Platonic Eros for life and teases himself (and the reader) with the possibility of an eternal cycle of life—an instinct strong in childhood, but covered over as we grow up. The notion of enjoying a previous life is, as he says, "far too shadowy a notion to be recommended to faith, as more than an element in our instincts of immortality." Nevertheless, there is nothing in faith to contradict the notion and even a favorable analogy for it in the story of the fall of Man. The fifth stanza of the Ode imagines the instinctual desire for life:

> Our birth is but a sleep and a forgetting;
> The soul that rises with us, our life's star,
> Hath had elsewhere setting
> And cometh from afar;
> Not in entire forgetfulness,
> And in not utter nakedness,
> But trailing clouds of glory do we come
> from God, who is our home:
> Heaven lies about us in our infancy!
> Shades of the prison house begin to close
> Upon the growing boy,
> But he beholds the light, and whence it flows,
> He sees it in his joy;
> The youth who daily farther from the east

Must travel, still is Nature's priest,
And by the vision splendid
Is on his way attended;
At length the Man perceives it die away,
And fade into the light of common day.

Finally, Keats, in his *Endymion*, recasts Diotima's lesson to Socrates of the ultimate object of human love—Absolute, unchanging, and Everlasting Beauty:

A thing of beauty is a joy forever:
Its loveliness increases; it will never
Pass into nothingness; but still will keep
A bower quiet for us, and a sleep
Full of sweet dreams, and health, and quiet
breathing.

Chapter Twenty-Five

Billy's Notebook Part X: Sexuality—The Dark Desires

Human beings have cloaked sexuality in a dark veil of mystery, guilt, and shame. Sexuality is the forbidden pleasure approached cautiously in literature, song, and myth and constrained by social orders representing legal and religious values. By many standards of good and decent societies, sex is barely tolerated. In spite of modern media avenues that approach sexuality with enticing quantities of "sex for sale," sex remains behind closed doors—in the closet of obscurity. Even as human sexuality is given such media prominence on television, tabloid papers, Internet web sites, it is still laden with a secret allure that skirts the mainstream of social approval. Indeed, the very appeal of media sex is the flirtation of tempting the viewer—as a voyeur—to defy social propriety by entering the secret lairs of surrogate sexual pleasures.

This shrouding of the most powerful of human desires is congruent with human history—at least the history that we identify as being a record of "civilization." As so many thinkers have pointed out, civilization, i.e., the orderly cooperation of human groups engaged in purporting to achieve a common success, exacts certain individual costs. It would seem that early in the formation of "civilized" groups, the members of social orders feared the most powerful desire of sexuality. They realized its constructive force necessary for the continuation of the society, but also its blinding power to obliterate reason in a self-seeking drive that temporally ignores any common good of the group.

Consider the Greek myth of Eros, the primordial god who came out of the egg that formed the earth (Gaea) and the heaven (Uranos). Eros embodies the demanding desire of sex that paralyzes even the gods in a frenzy of love that denies them rational decisions. His lustful love for the tender spirit, Psyche, can only be carried out in darkness and concealment. Sexual desire is a voracious beast that should never see the light of day. Only in darkness can Eros express his love for Psyche who innocently assumes that her unknown lover is a beast sent to have his way with her by the jealous Aphrodite. Praxitelus, the renowned fourth century BCE sculptor, represents Eros as forever hiding in the shadows—beneath the threshold of reason—ready to usurp reason's light with the dark desire. Nor can Eros ever be satisfied. He is born of Poverty and Resourcefulness—always contriving to fulfill the most powerful of desires but always failing to be fully satisfied. This pleasure-pain quandary entails a cruel sadomasochistic underside of human nature that civilization papers over with a thin veneer of sanity. The author Camille Paglia finds the roots of this double-sided desire in pagan religions that still peek through the accepted mainstream versions of religious belief.

> Sadomasochism is a sacred cult, a pagan religion that reveals the dark secrets of nature. The bondage of sadomasochism expresses our own bondage by the body, our subservience to its brute laws, concealed by our myths of romantic love.

Always standing opposed to reason—even when sex is sanctioned in marriage by the canons of civil society, sexual desire carries an overriding residue that this deeply sensual and egocentric desire has little semblance to the affectionate and tender love portrayed by an approving society. Society is ruled by laws of reason. Sexual desire is the antipathy of reason. The existential philosopher Jean Paul Sartre goes beyond the traditional battle lines of reason versus desire; he contends that sexual desire culminates in the very incarnation of consciousness in which one becomes a seducer turning the *spirit* of the other into flesh—at least for that brief intense moment. The sexual desire of consciousness "makes itself a body."

To understand this powerful notion of sexual desire, one must recapture Sartre's view of human consciousness that alone gives meaning to human existence through the many possibilities that the transparency of consciousness presents. Through consciousness, we are open to the world. We are not defined like inanimate objects. Our very knowledge points us to all other possible situations other than the physical one we are actually in. Through consciousness we are "pure possibilities" and, therefore, free and unique individuals. Sexual desire destroys that inanimate conscious freedom. Sexual desire is an overwhelming power that transforms a pure consciousness into a pure body. It is the caress—the touching of flesh upon flesh—that awakens sexual desire in the caressor and eventually transforms the one caressed into pure flesh. The one caressed is "captured" bodily and gives up her or his person to the pleasurable desires of the other. Physical mobility is one consequence of freedom, and it is precisely this bodily mobility that is taken by sexual desire. While not naming caressing "foreplay," Sartre suggests that the caressing of the fleshiest parts of the body initiates the "shiver of pleasure" that begins the seductive process of turning conscious thought into an immobile state of being. The overwhelming power of sexual desire moves one away from consciously chosen possibilities and toward a concrete and fixed entity. The sexual lover "appropriates" the other not as a person, but as a body. The other, now reduced by desire, to flesh or body, may be clothed and adorned by cosmetics and clothing, but it is really the body's movement that characterizes bodily existence. And it is that movement that sexual desire freezes in the heat of the passion. The stripping of the other's clothing is merely an external symbol of possessing the other. The possession consummates the desire when the other's consciousness is made bodily and immobile.

While Sartre's account of sexual desire might lead some to think he is describing a rape scene, Sartre suggests that this seductive "incarnation of the spirit" is characteristic of all sexual desires and sexual acts. He does contend that the "incarnation"—i.e., the transformation of conscious person into bodily entity—is reciprocal. The aggressor in this seduction of sex undergoes an incarnation himself (Sartre's use of pronouns indicates that the "possessor" is male; the one "possessed" is female). In order to experience the culmination of desire, the aggressive seducer undergoes a bodily transformation similar to that which the "other" is compelled to undergo—the compulsion being directed by sexual desire that makes it appear to be a "willing" compulsion.

Is this reciprocity of physical passion that Sartre describes in existential or phenomenological terms any more than what so many popular expressions name as a temporary out-of-control state of irrational sexual frenzy? Are *any* descriptions of sexual desire and passion compatible with the more romantic views of love and marriage that have become important foundations of society? Whatever our answer, there is something very powerful and dreadful about Sartre's philosophical analysis of sexual desire. *Powerful*, in his claim that sexual desire immobilizes the "other" in a seduction of control; *dreadful*, inasmuch as human consciousness is transformed into a physical condition—a thing. There is an inevitable interplay of sadistic and masochistic forces at work in all sexual urges. The desire to take hold and utterly control the other is the passion of sadism. Especially so, since at the inception of sexual desire, the appropriator resists becoming pure flesh.

> Sadism is an effort to incarnate the other through violence and this incarnation by force must be already the appropriation and utilization of the other. Sadism like desire seeks to strip the other of the acts which hide him. It seeks to reveal the flesh beneath the action.

Thus, sadism lurks behind every sexual desire to appropriate another *body* to the exclusion of conscious possibilities. Masochism is implied in the pleasurable yielding to appropriation and ultimate surrender to "being possessed."

This self-inflicted pleasure or pain quandary is expressed well in a brief scene from Alice McDermott's award winning novel *Charming Billy*. Two young adults meet on the beach of a summer resort and engage in a summer of confused promises, hopes, and deceptions. And as Sartre might suggest, conscious thought is made dense in the irrational pleasure of the moment.

"Think of the promises he made to Mary at moments when the girl had every right to believe him. When, for as long as it took, he managed to believe himself. With so many other forces at work in the world, brutal, sly, deceiving, unstoppable forces, what could be more foolish than staking your life on an ephemeral feeling, no more than an idea, really a fancy, the culmination of which is a clumsy bit of nakedness, a few minutes of animal grunting and bumping, a momentary obliteration of thought, of conscience?"

The dark furtiveness of sexual desire engenders an accompanying guilt or shame. One might claim that the degree of shame is proportionate to a society's claim to civility. Lawful society demands restraint of one's desires, especially of the most forceful sexual desire. Since the body in general is the locus of sexuality, and since the genitalia are the specific organs of sexuality, then the nakedness of the body is to be a public scandal and a personal shame. The Judaic-Christian tradition gets off the mark immediately with the shamefulness and guilt of one's naked body. Adam and Eve's idyllic life in the Garden, where "both the man and his wife were naked, but they felt no shame" was brought to a halt when God's edict to forego the fruit of the tree of knowledge was broken. They immediately become aware of their nude bodies and are ashamed.

Christianity codifies the guilt of sexual desire and/or intercourse through the powerful writings of Paul ("who will deliver me from this body of death!") and Augustine ("Give me chastity, Lord, but NOT YET!"). Both influential writers decry the "temptations of the flesh and can barely cope with the allure of sexual desire. Augustine, in his Confessions, chides himself for lack of control over his sexual passion. He fathers a child out of wedlock, renounces his profligacy, banishes his lover, and agrees to sanction sex through a respectable marriage to a good Christian maiden. Unfortunately, the girl is not yet of age, and Augustine, unable to postpone his sexual desire until the requisite time, takes up with another paramour. Intellectually convinced of what should be a better life for him as a Christian, he utters the above cry of desperation and shame for yielding to his overpowering sexual desires. His ultimate conversion and elevation to a high position in the Christian church and his influential voluminous writings assured a codified guilt attached to the dark desire of sex. Subsequent theological writings established total continence as the surest way through the heavenly gates, with marriage as a second best concession to those with less strong wills for saving their souls. Medieval writers created a substantive for human genitalia from a verb denoting shame and guilt: *Pudenda: of which one ought to be ashamed; disgraceful.*

The mass appeal of smutty jokes, pornographic writings and pictures, off-color references to private body parts are people's safety valves reducing the pressure of that dark desire constrained by the greater part of civil society. Higher forms of artistic endeavor to express the sexual dynamism of human nature in literature, painting, dance, and sculpture attain an acceptable status—often, however, when the artist is dead. Shame of sexual desire has been firmly established as religious, moral, and legal sanctions of all civil societies. Society fears the dark desire and strives to contain it. However, like Eros lurking in the shadows, sexual desire is always there as a powerful force lying beneath the mere veneer of civilization.

Chapter Twenty-Six

Parallel Worlds: One Straight, One Gay

It began with seemingly idle chatter between Gussie and Ernie sitting on the grassy bank along the third base line. It was the bottom of the third inning against the Spring Mill Blue Jays, and unless the Wildcats were in for a big inning, the two boys would probably not be up at bat.

"Do you think it is true?" asked Ernie quizzically.

"What?" answered Gussie, impatient with Ernie's persistence.

"That he is light in his loafers?"

"Yeah, but it is weird that he doesn't throw like a girl—or walk like one," Ernie countered.

They were talking about the opposing team's third baseman, Jonathon Foster, who was just out of earshot of the two Wildcats and had just made a nifty play on a hard hit ball by Big Joe. The big third baseman had made a backhand stab on the half-hop of a smash hit by Big Joe and threw him out a first.

Jon was a likeable, quiet kid who was respected by all the boys in the league as a darn good player. He had a classic stand-up batting stance and hit the ball for power. His defensive abilities as a third baseman were unquestioned. Not many balls got past Jon. No one knew how the word got around that Jonathon Foster was gay, but it did, in spite of the fact that the boys at this time in the social history of all things rumored could only relate a person's gayness to their physical behavior. Thus, Ernie's bewilderment in pegging Foster as gay if he did not "throw like a girl" nor exhibit any other of the stereotypical movements expected of gayness. "He didn't walk or run like a girl either," Ernie lamented.

Ernie and Gussie discussed this enigma about Jonathon in the brief conversation they had while their team was at bat. While he did not act gay, it was noted that he never attended any social functions involving girls—like the frequent school dances in the gym. And although, Jonathon was a member in good standing of the elite Hi Y Club, he would never sign on to go to any regional meetings where there were sure to be "red hot" meetings with the girls' counterpart to the boys' club, the Tri Hi Y. Those meetings were the talk of the boy's locker room, temporarily drawing away boys from Link-of-the-Locker- room's circle of curious delights. Returning Hi Y members would spin exaggerated yarns of nightly forays after formal business meetings to the third floor of the hotel where the girls were lodging. One wonders how naïve the adult citizen planners of this Young Men's Christian Association really were.

These were school-sanctioned trips that were not without cost. Much of the expenses were assumed by do-good civic groups like Kiwanis or Junior Chamber of Commerce or Rotary Clubs. The men who sponsored these statewide meetings for "outstanding" high school students were promoting the link between good business and good citizenship through Good Fellowship. Most of the business titans that supported these efforts were active members in their local masonic lodges and were sincerely convinced that good citizenship and good business were reciprocal terms. These boys could hope for no better goal in life to succeed in business and in turn become models of the community—as they themselves are. Maybe they did not realize that the majority of Hi Y members from the public school the Wildcats attended were blue-collar boys whose father worked the mills and factories of town. These boys would not know a Junior Mason from a Mason jar. They were actually more familiar with the latter, which their mothers used to preserve the tomatoes they grew. Did these paragons of virtue and good living know what their outstanding representatives did in the after-hours of their conventions? They tried to "make out" with female delegates from different parts of the state—from distances far enough from home so that embellished stories of male heroics could be never be validated or disputed. What the boys did not know was that the meetings of the adults at their own conventions would make the boys' claims seem like child's play.

Jonathon turned down every opportunity to represent his local Hi Y Club at these highly desirous ventures. He must be gay.

The ultimate nail that fastened the rumored label on this poor boy came from the local female population. Jonathon Foster was a good-looking kid—tall, with a square jaw, and dark wavy hair; he had a shy, winning smile and was never afflicted with the teenage kiss of death—acne. Many a girl had an adolescent crush on this young Adonis. They tried everything to get his attention and affection. Sally Bergey, the undisputed high school beauty, dropped her books as he walked by, feigning a frustration of a true damsel in distress. Jon smiled, gathered her books off the hall floor, politely returned them to her, and walked off. No invitation to meet later for a Coke at the local soda fountain, no invitation to go together to the school dance, no offer of a movie date to see the latest and hottest Veronica Lake and Alan Ladd movie at the Riant Theater. Many a romance began at those Saturday night pictures. The fact that Sally, the number one seeded beauty, failed to win over handsome Jon did not discourage a whole contingent of girls to gain the attention of this intractable young man. Nothing worked. They all failed. And it was from the female side of the gym locker areas that the word came out that Jonathon Foster must be gay. The whisper down the lane drill is infallible: "Do you think he might be gay?"

"Someone thinks Jon is Gay."

"Naomi wondered if Jon was gay."

"June said that Jon is gay."

"Have you heard the *definite* news?" Jonathon Foster is gay.

What confused most in this closeted age of hidden homosexuals was the undeniably observed fact that Jonathon did not act gay. This was Ernie's puzzlement. Everyone knew how gay men acted.

Just look around. Little Jimmy Roberts, the ninth grader in Gussie's homeroom, was gay. As Gussie put it, "He *was* light in his loafers." He sashayed when other boys walked. He was the last picked in a gym class volleyball game because he had no coordination and was generally very poor at athletics. He preferred art and music over basketball and baseball. He reversed the age-old tactic of males trying to attract females. Jimmy talked mostly to girls in the hall while casting side glances at the boys. Straight boys did the opposite. Everybody knew this, and they pretty much accepted Jimmy for what he was. No one picked on Jimmy, but it did not stop the boys from using language that would be demeaning to boys of a homosexual orientation. Without ever being aware that they might be hurting him, they would use the familiar terms *queer, fairy, fag*. Jimmy would look away and try to change the subject, helpless to make them aware of something he could not understand himself. Why was he different from the other boys?

Jimmy probably exhibited the most obvious characteristics that labeled him with different sexual proclivities, but he wasn't the only male that bore the indicting social stigma. Frederick Cartwright was the tenth-grade math teacher at the high school. He was a good teacher but, quite obviously, in the terms of his students, "weird." His effete gestures were not as pronounced as Jimmy's, but they were there and were obvious to an observant classroom of youngsters all too eager to pounce on any morsel of perceived defect in an authority figure. The way he handled the chalk when he did his math calculations on the black board; his weak, limp-wrist handshake when he congratulated students at academic assemblies; his lack of a firm physique that bordered on being somewhat flabby—all contributed to the conclusion that Mr. Cartwright was different—in a sexual way. The students cruelly referred to Mr. Cartwright as F to the second power, or F Squared, which was their unthinking teen code for "Freddy Fairy." Whenever any math problem went up on the board involving squared numbers, the class would erupt in raucous laughter that totally disrupted and confused the innocent teacher who would attempt a weak questioning smile suggesting that he would laugh too even if he did not get the joke. His feeble attempt to relate to the humor prolonged the classroom chaos. Once, during a square root joke in Mr. Cartwright's class, Mr. Goebel, the stern principal, was patrolling the corridors and passed the door at the moment of loud laughter. Mr. Goeble was of the old German school that laughter and learning did not mix, and assuming that Cartwright had lost control of his class, he quickly opened the door. Goebel's presence evoked immediate silence whether he was presiding at an assembly or prowling the corridors. He was more feared than loved by both students and teachers. "What is going on in here, Mr. Cartwright?" Poor Mr. Cartwright mumbled something about his feeble attempt to pun with the word *Pi*, and that he was totally responsible for the breech of classroom decorum and all is well now. "I certainly hope so," growled the towering *Schulmeister*, as he glared menacingly at the cowering students. The kids in the class actually felt sorry for poor Freddy squared over this humiliating experience, and they actually did temper their mocking humor of him.

Careful observers of folks like Jon Foster and Jimmy Roberts and Frederick Cartwright would notice that they were living two lives. The one life where they interacted with those who considered themselves "normal" and a separate life of social contact with those majority of people who thought them to be abnormal. The majority never knew of their hidden lives. They interacted on the ball field, the classroom, the places of employment, but they did so as a masquerader at a costume party. Their mask had to be always on. The sad truth is that some were given better disguises than others. Jonathon Foster was gay, but when the girls began that rumor, they really did not mean it. Their charges were an expression of hurt feelings and wounded pride in not being chosen by this handsome young man. Calling him "gay" was a generic insult equivalent to "stupid" or "ugly." They never literally believed he was gay because his actions and appearances did not fit the stereotypical expectations of being gay. Jon wore the mask of a straight man very well.

Jimmy, on the other hand, had no disguise at all. He was definitely seen as a caricature of a human being, an occasional provider of comic relief for the boys bored by the classroom routines or the required calisthenics of the gym class. He bore the brunt of ridicule and exclusion, especially from what teen boys need the most—peer acceptance in the games they play, the jokes they tell, and the risks they take. He had none of that.

Mr. Cartwright could never gain the full respect of the classroom because his slight but definitely effete mannerisms overshadowed any equation he wrote on the board. He could never sell his discipline as being a valuable life lesson because he could not sell himself. The students were not buying because he did not conform to the preconceived ideal of human nature. But Cartwright was old enough and wise enough to know what was going on. He was past the teen years and had accepted and embraced the parallel life he was forced to live. He found love and companionship in a hidden world that was totally different from the place he occupied in that public school where he was viewed as a somewhat feckless misfit. He was smart enough—to be sure—he knows math, doesn't he? But his demeanor in public was "gay enough" to make him lose the respect of the boys he hoped to educate. If the boys had ever seen Mr. Cartwright with his gay peers at the social clubs he frequented, they would have seen an unrecognizable "F squared"—a man of confidence and competence.

Such was the separate world that gays were forced to inhabit. One in which they demonstrated completely different *personae* from the ones displayed in their professions or schools. It was a parallel world that Jimmy Roberts would soon find, and one that Jon Foster tragically denied.

Jonathon Foster eventually yielded to the social pressure that so wanted him to be the person he appeared to be on the surface. The pressure was mounted from every social institution that came to bear on the unfortunate young man. His family urged him quietly but persistently to "do things that every boy seems to do." They wondered if he met any nice girls at school. He was in his senior year in high school and showed no interest in dating. Was he going to go to his senior prom? "Why don't you ask that nice Bergey girl?" Life at school with his peers and persistent flirtations from the girls was reaching a point where the boy had to make some decisions. The church that Jon and his family attended was a very conservative Protestant Fundamentalist house of worship where the Holy Bible

—every word of it—was directly from the mouth of God. Jon's parents enlisted the aid of Pastor Walker to speak with Jon. The good pastor assured his parents that there was nothing wrong with Jon that a lovely Christian girl from their church couldn't cure—within the Graces of God's Holy Matrimony, of course. Give him time, Pastor Walker reassured them.

Jon eventually did marry soon after graduating from a Christian college where he majored in accounting and met the ideal mate envisioned by his parents and his pastor. Susan Wright was a shy, attractive girl majoring in elementary education, and she shared Jon's religious views that God's laws were unambiguously stated in the good book and that no human law or mortal contract could ever countermand the Will of the Divine.

There seemed little doubt that Jonathon Foster sincerely believed that his sexual condition was an affliction from either a god who tested him or a devil who tempted him and that marriage to a good Christian girl would cure him of this tormenting disease. After graduation, Jon and Susan married. Jon got a good job with a major accounting firm. Susan, pregnant with their first child—a boy, Jonathon Jr.—quit her teaching job to raise her child as a good mother and wife should do. A second child was born a few years later. They purchased a lovely home in the suburbs. Jon got several promotions, and after fifteen years of living an unholy lie, Jonathon Foster left his family. No one knows what happened to him. A real American tragedy born of ignorance and socially constructed bigotry by a population that confuses a majority number with normality. Jon had the misfortune of being born too soon. Had society's changes happened earlier in this man's life, he never would have married Susan and committed both of them to a senseless charade of false hope and the flimsy veneer of being the perfect American family.

Some of the boys of the Sixth Avenue Wildcats lived to witness one of the most amazing social and political changes in the history of humankind—if only for the rapid pace of the changes. The forced parallel lives of gay people were breaking down as they moved into the mainstream of society through the legal actions of the courts and the concomitant changes in social attitudes. De jure and de facto acceptance prevailed with great alacrity in both marriage and employment equality for gays who emerged from the closets in great numbers.

Billy brought up the subject of same-sex attraction in a conversation with his mother. He reiterated part of the talk that Gussie and Ernie had started about Jon Foster. Billy's mom was a single-minded person of the live-and-let-live school. She did not pretend for Billy's behalf that she understood same-sex attraction, but she was keenly aware of many acquaintances who "leaned in that direction." She even mentioned a few relatives who fit "that category" very nicely. Of course, no one in the extended family ever mentioned it or, for that matter, ever treated them any differently from other family members. It was an unwritten code of silence and tacit denial by avoidance. It is not a problem if you never say it is a problem. Billy's family was the precursor to "don't ask, don't tell."

His mom did get more animated, however, when she talked of Grace Butera, a neighbor who lived only two blocks away. Grace raised two boys pretty much by herself. Her husband left the family after seven years of marriage. He was gay, and Grace tried to have the marriage annulled by the church. Billy's mom was no canon lawyer, to be sure, and only knew the neighborhood gossip that said Grace was denied an annulment because she duly received the Sacrament of Holy Matrimony in the church service, and her two boys were living proof that the marriage was consummated. Grace eventually remarried but was denied access to the normal services in the very church where she was baptized and married. Billy's mother relayed this last bit of news with more than a hint of contempt in her voice that reflected the opinion of most rank-and-file Catholics—that the right connections and sufficient funds could annul any Catholic dogma. All the good folks of St. Anthony's Parish knew that the church's biggest benefactor married a second wife after divorcing his first. The church, in this case, declared the first marriage null and void according to canon law. Was it a coincidence that Sam D'Orio, who obtained the annulment, was the wealthiest man in the parish? Sam was a successful real estate agent and a most prominent member of the community whose beneficence was evident in the new recreation center and in the addition to the town library. His generosity to his church was duly inscribed in marble on the main altar of St. A's church. Everyone at Mass could read it as they went to the communion rail: GIFT OF SAMUEL W. D'ORIO AND FAMILY. The good parishioners of St. A's often joked as to which family gave the generous gift, the first or second?

Billy's mom would never know the fate of Jon and Susan Foster's failed attempt at marriage, but in her own time, she knew the sorrow of Grace Butera, who, along with her husband, was a victim of the church's pressure, which brought so much misery to their lives. And to add insult to injury, the church denied Grace, one of the faithful, the comfort of its healing rituals. When her sons were grown and on their own, Grace Butera took her own life.

Billy remembered the many times his mother recounted to family members Grace's story and how his mother could never understand how the church could be so hardened and indifferent to the suffering of good people. As an aging senior citizen, Billy marveled that so many attitudes and laws would change within his own generation over same-sex attraction. It was in those recalcitrant strongholds of organized religions that strident opposition continued, even as illogical and irrelevant that resistance may be. He wondered how different and how much better would have been the lives of Jon Foster, Jimmy Roberts, Fred Cartwright, and Grace Butera, and the millions of gay people if those churches practiced the love they preached.

Chapter Twenty-Seven

Softball? Yes, the Church Softball League

There was a younger age when no respecting Wildcat team member would play *softball*. It was a fake, a poor imitation, a downright degradation of America's pastime. With its shrunken field, obscene enlarged ball, an added player positioned somewhere between the outfield and infield, thus eliminating the perfectly placed "Texas League" single, "well, it's a game for girls—and old men."

It was thought among the more-youthful aspirants with ambitions to play in the big leagues that playing softball would ruin all the wonderful skills needed to play the real game of ball. There may or not be any logic to the charges leveled against the game of softball by the true aficionados of "hard ball." The rules are basically the same—and yes, the base paths are shortened, the ball bigger, and a "short fielder" catches what the outfield and infield players can't. But it is, fundamentally, the same game, requiring the same variety of skills of the parent game. Unlike the game of golf, for example, where one learns to repeat in exactly the same way a robot-like swing at a tiny ball. It is the design of the club that determines the destiny of the ball's trajectory. The longer the club and the flatter the face will increase the distance and decrease the height; the shorter the club and more open the face decreases the distance and increases the height.

The body motion of the swing never changes; the club does the rest. Imagine a player fooling around with the composition and design of a baseball bat. Those who tried it in the past found themselves playing ball in the Mexican League! Now, these may be simplistic comparisons that many golfers would deem unfair. Baseball bats do vary in length and weight and handle thickness, but the facts remain. Baseball requires a plethora of skills—running, throwing, fielding, hitting—that is unique among athletic endeavors. One need not be the fastest kid on the block, but be blessed with strength and eye coordination to hit that tantalizing sphere of a ball with a round bat. Ernie could do that. One might not be the biggest kid in the class, but had the speed to beat out infield grounders, hit more line drive singles than Ernie would hit home runs. Billy could do that. It is a game that embraces a multitude of talents, without demanding absolute perfection in any one of those talents. Baseball is different.

Whether or not the aging Wildcats rationalized their playing in the local church-organized softball league by recognizing that it was still a baseball game, or whether their diminishing skills welcomed the shortened field and the larger ball, is not known. But there they were representing the church that baptized, confirmed, and married them—and will probably bury them—on a softball field.

They had other "adult" responsibilities now. Most were married; some had kids. Reds was still the unofficial leader of the team, designating the position that each played, setting the batting order to effect the maximum run production. He was also demonstrating his unobtrusive leadership at the steel mill where he worked since graduating high school. He was elected as shop steward of the local union. Reds demonstrated the same fairness and even temperedness in the thorny area of labor-management issues as he did with his ball players. Ernie worked there as well. Big Joe drove a truck. Gussie worked as a bank clerk. And Billy was teaching high school social studies that he learned from Mr. Driedger. They were all pretty much the same—a little older, a little slower, a lot more tolerant of softball, "the game of old men and girls."

They played in the town's official "Church Softball League" organized by a committee of representatives from each of the seven churches in town—five Protestant churches and two Roman Catholic. This league was not to be taken lightly. The election of the team representatives to the "commission" was given as much serious thought as electing the town's mayor. The commission was responsible for setting and enforcing not only the rules governing the play on the field, but other important issues such as player eligibility and proper decorum on the playing field and "all adjacent areas." The official league rule book was the product of a commission whose members were "in good standing with their respective churches and not playing members of their respective teams." Every other year, a commissioner was elected from candidates recommended by their pastors. Reds once joked when asked if he knew who was elected to this awesome responsibility of overseeing a small-town softball league, "I don't think the election is over. I haven't seen any white smoke coming from the Vatican yet."

It was no laughing matter, however, when it came to publishing the rule book—especially the section on "proper decorum on the playing field and all adjacent areas." The member representing St. Paul's Baptist Church wanted to ban all alcoholic beverages from not only the ice chests that players placed next to the benches, but also from any containers brought by the family and friends sitting on the wooden bleachers. The commission member from St Matthew's Methodist Church declared a no-vote of games scheduled for Sunday afternoon, heading off any possible conflict with celebrating the Lord's Day.

All the issues that seemed rather trivial to Reds and the others were finally resolved, the league was formed, the official Rules of the Church Softball League written, and the season started.

The former Sixth Avenue Wildcats played for St. Anthony of Padua and wore the league-required full uniforms bearing the colors of their respective team. St. Anthony's colors were maroon and gray—long gray pants, maroon shirts with SAINTS emblazoned at the chest, and maroon caps with simply "ST A's" on the front. Compared to the simple white T-shirts upon which the boys' moms affixed the Wildcat decals, these uniforms were quite stylish. In spite of themselves, the grown-up Sixth Avenue gang enjoyed the softball games as much as they could. And they were good at it, although deep down they knew it wasn't the same as their Wildcat days. Really! Adults playing bastard baseball! Yes, the uniforms were a marked improvement over a pair of jeans and a white shirt, but so many things were different. Even the sound of the bat striking the ball was annoying. It was no longer "the sharp crack of the bat." It was more like a dull thud. Imagine a baseball announcer calling an exciting play on the radio, "And the runners were off at the thud of the bat!"

Nevertheless, with only a week left until the end of the first summer season, St. A's was in second place, a full game ahead of St. George's Episcopal Dragons, and only a half game behind the league leading St. Stanislaus Barons. They were scheduled to play St. Stan's on Thursday at six in the evening. It was the last game of the season, and the league championship was on the line. The Barons was the other Catholic Church team in the league. The church was founded as an ethnic Polish church to serve the immigrants who came from Poland to work in the mills and factories alongside of the Italian immigrants who attended St. Anthony's. Both Poles and Italians, as children, attended the same public school—having no church-sponsored school of their own. The players knew each other very well, playing as teammates on the high school sports. There was one player, however, on St. Stanislaus' team that was unknown to the former Wildcats. He was their pitcher by the name of Pete Johnson. In fact, in a small town in which everybody knew everybody, *nobody* seemed to know Pete Johnson. This would not be a very significant matter if it were not for the fact that this mystery man was the reason St. Stan's was in first place near the end of the season. Pete Johnson pitched in a style like no other softball pitcher at this time in the short history of this pretender to the game. He was a windmill pitcher and was practically unhittable. Every softball pitcher, at this time, threw in the classic underhand motion. Some could throw the large ball with some significant speed. But the fast ball in soft ball was merely a change-up to the slower and trickier back-spin ball or slower in-curve ball that was analogous to the screw ball of big league hard ball. Pete Johnson had no change-up. He threw fast, faster, and fastest. He would kick his left leg high and straight in front of his body and wheel his right arm around in a 360-degree arc, releasing the ball with tremendous velocity from a mere forty-six feet from mound to home plate. He was wild enough to prevent batters from digging in at the plate and controlled enough to issue few walks. He led the league in strikeouts.

It might sound strange to those who watch on TV today the wonderful women athletes competing in the college softball games where all the pitchers have perfected the windmill style of challenging the hitters. So what was the big deal about Pete Johnson? It was a big deal and only those who deny it are oblivious to the importance of history and change and development and all the other factors that contribute to the wisdom of the ages. Wisdom is said to come with age, but this is not necessarily true. The aged can be foolish and the young can be wise. It depends on what ideals they employ in understanding reality. It is foolish to think that softball began with the LSU women's softball team simply because that is the first softball game the person witnessed. It is equally foolish to think that aviation began with supersonic jets because no one remembers the Wright Brothers. Believe it! Pete Johnson was a scary anomaly of the Church Softball League. He threw a windmill fast ball. And the men of St. A's were facing him for the league championship late Thursday afternoon.

There was something else about this mystery man that was somewhat intimidating. He never wore a glove or a baseball cap. He played bare-handed, as if to say, "You're never going to hit the ball, so I will never have to catch it." His hatless head was adorned with slick black hair that was never out of place. It was as if he had just stepped out of the shower and neatly parted and combed his hair—never to be mussed again. He always had the same stoic facial expression except with the slightest hint of a curled-lip cynical sneer. He never seemed to fraternize with his teammates before or after games. It was suspected that a few members of the "proper decorum" committee wanted to force Pete to wear a hat and use a glove. Other representatives of the "legitimate church membership" committee were approached asking whether Pete was really a member of St. Stanislaus. After all, he wasn't even Polish. Was he? Nothing came from these alleged investigations of Pete Johnson, so here we are, St.

A's and St. Stan's facing off in the final game of the season. The winner takes home the trophy.

The game was, without doubt, the best game of this summer softball league played by men coming very close to the down side of their athletic days. Reds slotted himself in the line up to pitch for the A's. Reds played shortstop when he wasn't pitching—the same versatility he showed as a hard-ball playing Wildcat, but in softball, Reds was a wily underhand tosser that fooled the batters with guile and deception. Back hand spinners reversed off the bat as infield pop-ups, curving sliders that came out of the side of his hand were easy ground outs, big exaggerated motion that resulted in a slow change-up off the plate, but tempting enough to prompt swings that were way out in front of the ball were strike outs, sneaky fast balls that were preceded by hardly any exaggerated motion—and then the ball exploded upon the batter were late swing put outs. All smoke and mirrors from a very cagy athlete who adjusted well to this new way of playing baseball.

On the other side, Pete Johnson was doing his thing, overpowering the men from St. A's. He had seven strikeouts and only allowed two walks through the first six innings. St. A's had their best shot at him in the third inning. He had retired the first six batters, but walked Ernie and Gussie with two outs in the top of the third. Big Joe was up next and worked a full count on Johnson, who seemed uncharacteristically perturbed. Careful observation of the usually unflappable pitcher would reveal slight beads of perspiration on his hatless forehead. Maybe he was vulnerable after all. There was a stir of expectation among the few family and friends of St. A's who were seated on the rickety bleachers along the third base line. Reds said a few words to Big Joe from his coaching box at third base, and St. A's best power hitter dug in at the batter's box. The big slugger patiently fouled off some marginal pitches, laid off obviously bad pitches, and managed to work a full count on a now obviously annoyed Pete Johnson. It was only the third inning, but St. A's might not get this good a chance against this pitcher. With the count 3 and 2, the runners ran with the release of the ball as Big Joe caught a fast ball late and drove it deep in the alley between right and center field. The ball began to curve sharply toward right as St. Stan's right fielder ran toward it and made a leaping backhanded catch of the ball. Inning over. Reds called encouragement to his teammates as they took the field, telling them that they would do better next inning, and he also congratulated the opposing right fielder as he ran in from his position. Reds was like that.

Now it was the bottom of the sixth inning of a seven-inning softball game, and there was still no score. This was very unusual for a game with such a big ball to hit. The combination of Pete Johnson's windmill fast ball and Red's crafty pitching, along with excellent fielding plays on the part of both teams, accounted for the scoreless deadlock. St. Stan's had been designated the home team, and in the bottom of the sixth with two outs, Reds gave up his first base-on-balls. The next batter singled through the hole between short and third. Men on first and second, two outs, and St. Stan's big left fielder, Eddie Stemporoski up at the plate. He wasted no time and picked on Reds's first pitch, an attempt to sneak a fast ball on the outside corner. Eddie drove the ball to the gap in right center field. The runner on second scored easily, but Billy got to the ball quickly as the man on first was rounding third and heading for home. In one motion, Billy scooped the ball and threw a one-hopper to Ernie who made a sweeping tag on the runner. The inning was over, but the damage was done. St. A's had one more chance in the top of the seventh against Pete Johnson, who swaggered out to the mound with restored confidence. After six and a half innings, St. Stan's led by the slim margin of 1–0.

In the top of the seventh, last chance for St. A's, it did not look good. Ernie got some power on a Pete Johnson pitch but got under it and hit a towering pop-up to the third baseman. Gussie batted next and hit a sharp grounder to the left of short and was thrown out by a half a-step by the shortstop who made a good back handed stab of the ball. Since Reds was pitching, he humbly put himself last in the batting order and was the remaining hope of keeping the game alive. He noticed that St. Stan's short fielder was playing on the left side of the field in the exact spot that Reds had smacked a single in a previous inning. Reds patiently waited for his pitch. He let two inside pitches go by and swung a bit late—on purpose, at an outside pitch that he could direct over the second baseman's head into right field for a single. Reds could do that. He handled the bat like a magician's wand. Tying run on first, two outs in the top of the seventh inning. St. A's lead-off hitter, Billy, stepped to the plate.

As he did as a youngster with the Sixth Avenue Wildcats, Billy batted in the first spot. He was the lead-off hitter for several good reasons: He had a good eye for the strike zone and walked a lot, he made good contact with the ball and rarely struck out, he was an exceptionally fleet runner, and he beat out many a ground balls for hits. The one thing he lacked was power. Most of his hits were singles, and the extra base hits that he did get were mainly because of his speed. Billy approached the hitter's box knowing what he had to do. His team was down by one run in the last inning with two outs against them. He had to extend the inning. He had to get on base and put Reds on second and in scoring position to tie the game. Pete Johnson showed streaks of wildness in this championship game, and Billy had every intention of working him for a base-on-balls. Reds, standing on the first base bag, gave Billy a knowing nod as he stepped to the plate. They were both thinking the same unspoken thought, "Work him for a walk."

Pete Johnson was also wise in the ways of the game. He knew that the last thing he wanted was to give Billy a free pass and put the tying run on second. He seemed flushed with a sudden rush of adrenalin. His face got red as he gripped the ball hard in both bare hands and stepped on the rubber. He stared at Billy and released the ball at the end of his whirlwind motion with greater velocity than any other pitch he threw so far. The ball dissected the plate and was belt high. "Strike one," the umpire bellowed, and Billy stepped out of the box. The next pitch was in the exact same spot—maybe with even greater speed. Strike two. Pete Johnson never stepped off the rubber and never took his eyes off Billy as he waited for him to face the third pitch. His stare became a contemptuous glare. It was clear that Johnson was not going to waste any time getting Billy to chase a bad pitch, or nibble at the corners of the plate hoping for a favorable call from the umpire. Johnson was going to blow Billy away with everything he had. Billy knew it and Reds knew it as he again glanced at Billy from first base and nodded in the direction of the outfield. "Hit it, Billy. Hit it hard and knock that smirk off that son-of-a-bitch's face." That was what the cartoon balloon said that was drawn above Red's serious face that Billy read.

Billy got back in the box, and Pete Johnson, with the same powerful motion, delivered the same high-velocity pitch right down the middle of the plate and belt high. Billy swung and made contact. It was a perfectly timed swing in which the middle of the bat met the middle of the ball at the middle of the plate. Billy's bat was the perfect extension of his arms—as if arms and bat were one. The rotation of Billy's hips, in synch with his shoulders and legs, created the exact torque of power that sent the ball soaring over the left fielder's head. It was a perfect swing. The stunned outfielder had been playing Billy shallow to begin with, but even at regular depth, he never would have caught that ball. In addition to the swing that Billy put on that ball, Sir Isaac Newton's third Law of Motion was also helping. "To every action there is an equal and opposite reaction." Billy's perfect swing provided the timing; Pete Johnson's arrogant speed provided the power. Billy never hit a ball that far before and would never hit one that hard again. By the time the startled fielder ran down the ball on the very edge of the park, Reds had crossed the plate with the tying run and Billy was rounding third, waved home by an enraptured Big Joe who was coaching at third. Billy crossed the plate standing up. No one remembers who made the third out that inning, but St. A's took the field for the bottom of the seventh with a 2–1 lead, three outs away from the first Church Soft Ball League championship.

The character of the men of St. A's is best appreciated by witnessing what happened after Billy hit that tremendous homer. By the time Billy got back to the bench where one would expect him to be mobbed by ecstatic teammates, Reds had given the signal to the rest of the team to ignore Billy in the time-honored silent treatment suggesting that what Billy did was not extraordinary and, in fact, was very much expected of him. They shunned him, walked away, and pretended to be preoccupied with more important items. The funny part of this epic scene was that Billy did not catch on to what they were doing. He was so stunned at what he had just done that he couldn't possibly catch the joke. Finally, Reds called off the ruse, and they mobbed a surprised Billy, wrestling him to the ground in celebration and acting as the Sixth Avenue boys they used to be.

The bottom of the seventh inning was anticlimactic. The Barons went down meekly in order. Reds was even more steely-eyed than Pete Johnson. He retired the first batter on a pop-up to third, the second on a routine fly to left, and got the final batter to hit a grounder back to the mound where Red gloved it and threw him out at first. The league threw a party that night celebrating the end of a successful first year for the Church Softball League. The party was pre-arranged to be held—no matter who won the game—at St. Stanislaus' Parish Hall. Since almost all of the players from both churches knew each other from the same public school they attended, they shared many laughs about their school days and embellished on many past stories. They all had transitioned from boyhood to manhood, from baseball to softball, and some of them wondered if, soon, they would be moving on to Slo-Pitch Softball. None of them did. Most played a few more years in the Church Softball League and then yielded to younger players. Their playing days were over.

Chapter Twenty-Eight

The Bottom of the Ninth

The Wildcats were pretty much a toothless bunch of old men now—"senior citizens," a euphemism for "difficult to get out of an easy chair after watching TV for two hours." Their baseball is limited to watching games on television and occasionally going to the town's Little League Park to watch their grandchildren play ball. The park was well manicured and maintained and was a far cry from the converted cow pasture that the Wildcats played on. There were actual fences enclosing the outfield, a screened backstop behind home plate, real bases instead of pieces of card board, and most impressive of all, kid-size dugouts made of concrete with players' benches inside. Of course, all the Little Leaguers had real baseball uniforms, which the League provided. Nothing was left to chance—even paid, black-uniformed umpires officiated the games. Little League was invented, organized, and managed exclusively by adults. All of these recent facets of the kids' game did not stop the old-timers from watching the kids play, however. Even more enjoyable was to play catch with the grandkids after Sunday dinner, when they came over to visit. Grandpop would find the old glove, a bat, and ball and go out in the backyard. Once, Billy said to his grandson, Zach, that they have a game of pepper. "Pepper, what's that Grandpop? I want to play baseball," Zach replied.

Sometimes, when watching the little league games at the park, they would reflect back on their own youthful baseball days and their

own initiative in making it all happen independent of any adult intervention. These flashbacks would occur, perhaps, whenever a cohort
of adults supervising the boys would admonish the youngsters who
may not have been playing up to the expectations of the adults. Billy
had such a recollection of a game in which Reds's father unexpectedly
showed up in the middle of one of their games and solemnly sat down
on the grassy bank along the third base line. Shortly after his arrival,
Billy had been caught in a rundown between second and third base.
He was trying to stretch a double into a triple and it didn't work. He
was trapped between the bases, but his quickness made it difficult for
the Blue Jay fielders to tag him out. He maneuvered back and forth
between the bases for what seemed an endless time and finally collapsed from near exhaustion and was tagged out. It was the final out
of the inning, and Billy and the other team ran off the field laughing.
All of the kids were laughing. It was comical, reminding the kids of
a slap stick movie scene from films they saw at the Riant Theater. As
they ran off the field laughing, Reds's father stood up, dusted off his
pants, and shouted out, "It's not funny." Well, the laughter stopped.
Everyone got silent. Reds was embarrassed. The rest of the game was
played out pretty much in sullen silence. All the fun was gone. After
the game, as the boys were at Jessie's drinking their usual milkshakes
with less than the usual enthusiasm because of the admonishment
over not taking their beloved game seriously enough, Big Joe broke
the unspoken tension by mimicking Reds's father, "It's not funny." It
became a mantra at many future games whenever the boys needed to
remind themselves that they needed a laugh.

When watching the little leaguers, they would also feel a pang
of discomfort whenever a youngster, fully uniformed in catcher's paraphernalia, would stick out his hand behind his back, requesting a
new ball from a fully uniformed umpire. It was also a bit painful to
watch a youngster step into the batting box and immediately hold
up a hand to the umpire, signaling that he was not quite ready and
that he would tell the ump when the pitcher could throw the ball.
It seemed a petty peeve on the part of the oldsters, but the gesture
of the kids was done every time, and with every batter. It seemed
canned or, worse, coached. That was one coaching technique that

never would have occurred to Reds. It was an affectation. And if there was anything attached to the brand of baseball played by the now ancient Sixth Avenue Wildcats, it was not acts of affectation. Watching the Little Leaguers in their uniforms playing with a ready supply of bats and balls, having umpires officiating the game, the old men could not help reflecting back on their own homemade league. And how they sold old newspapers and took the neighbors' trash to the town dump to earn money for the precious few bats and balls they used in their games. They remembered how they formed the neighborhood league without even adult knowledge, let alone supervision. And here on the manicured field in front of them, the adults supervising the game were more prominent to an outside viewer than were the players. The men were the more vocal ones—barking out instructions to the kids, "Wait for your pitch, Tommy—good eye, good eye." Shouting encouragement when needed, "You'll catch the next one, Frankie—shake it off, shake it off."

"C'mon, Mark, make him a hitter, get it over the plate."

This is the time-honored baseball chatter that used to come from Reds and his teammates. The boys on the field today didn't say much at all. It seemed to the old-timers that there were two games going on. One being played for the adult supervisors—played nervously by the boys who were acutely aware of playing to please them and trying not to make mistakes, and another shadow game that could only be perceived by viewers who were aware of other times when the game was played by kids. In this hidden game, the youngsters would quietly comfort their mate who erred, slap a silent happy teammate on the back after he made a nice play while the adult manager was instructing someone else, pump a silent fist in joyful satisfaction at something that only the boy knew he accomplished well and to his satisfaction. Watch the boys closely and a careful observer will see this covert game that the kids are playing all by themselves. This double vision was only visible to those who had played the other way and could now compare.

These feelings and thoughts of the oldsters as they watched today's youth playing organized ball should not be misunderstood. They were not in any way resentful of the opportunities the kids had of playing with a good supply of bats and balls on a beautifully prepared field. Or even to have men organize the league and instruct the boys in a way the former players never were. Not at all. There was not a hint of envy or jealousy. They were either too wise or too old for that nonsense. What they witnessed provoked in them a strong and sincere acknowledgment that "the times they were a changin'." They were keenly aware of the relentless movement of time. Very few people alive today could relate to how they played the game in their day—their day of playing the game was past. And yet it was the same game. There is the paradox that they perceived. "The more things change, the more they stay..." You know the cliché so there is no use beating a dead... "Stop using clichés," Tom said *predictably*.

It was, indeed, the same game, but viewed from different points of space and time. The kids on the field had more to see of the game by looking forward; the old men in the stands had more to see by looking backward. Einstein had it right; space and time are relative to the observer. Maybe to the kids today, the shape of the game was curved and warped into the way the boys played; just as from outer space the earth appears to be a small round marble, but to those down on earth, it is flat and straight. The Sixth Avenue Wildcats were of the earth. They grabbed fistfuls of dirt, not angel dust to rub on the bat handle to give them a better grip. They 'circled' the base paths on a flat plane until they reached home, their original starting point. The game ran along a straight line to the end. They were not resentfully wishing an impossible cyclic return to their youthful playing days, as they watched the kids today. They knew it was still the earthbound game they played and learned a lot about human relations and life itself by playing baseball. They had enough confidence in the game to feel that the kids today would learn the same lessons they had learned—even if those lessons were delayed a bit because of the too many decisions on the field made for the kids by the adults. They were having fun watching the kids play their game, even as they knew that their lives were on an inevitable straight line toward the end.

Chapter Twenty-Nine

Billy's Notebook Part XI: The Game of Sports—Living Life on Our Terms

O *ne of the last entries in Billy's Notebook offers a view of athletic games as a defiant human endeavor to challenge the inevitable end that nature has planned for us. Nature's inexorable laws care only for the continuation of the species and contemptuously shucks off individuals after a relatively short period of time. The human species, with its conscious awareness of this cruel natural indifference, create games governed by man-made rules that declares that human endeavors can win in games of their own making, and even if they lose in the contests, they can play another day. Sports are a temporary but important reprieve from the finality of life. As Billy puts it, "Athletics is not a metaphor for life. It is an alternative to life."*

The Meaning of Playing Sports

The games we commonly recognize as athletic contests originate in the fascinating spirit of play that lies so deeply within the human psyche. Play is that general human desire to be free from the arduous rigors of life, to engage in momentary periods of relief from socially imposed rules and regulations, to recreate oneself for no apparent reason except the sheer enjoyment of having fun. Play, in its purest form, is the spontaneous assertion of one's personal identity through a lighthearted defiance and rejection of all in society that represents externally imposed structure and order. In this most radical meaning of released self-expression, play can never be dictated by obligation or duty to perform in a fixed way, at an appointed time, in a definite place. Everyone has experienced this desire for impromptu action of play that takes us away from our ordinary and routine obligations: We decide on the spur of the moment to go bowling with a friend. We go for a solitary walk in the park for no other reason than it is a beautiful day and we want to enjoy the fresh air. On a whim, we sign up for a weekend of skiing. These natural pursuits of individual enjoyment are free from the highly structured forms of play that we recognize in organized athletic events. The spontaneous playtime of individuals is not taken seriously, is rarely conducted with an intense purpose of achievement, and is not viewed as a contest to determine winners and losers. However, expressions of *play* as organized formal events of athletics are highly competitive contests, not taken lightly by either participants or spectators, and —in many case—having a great amount of glory and riches accruing to the winners. While these are marked differences between the care-free play of individuals seeking recreational relief from life's burdens and the intense rigor of organized sporting events, nevertheless, it is the same spirit that energizes both manifestations of human beings at play. The question, then, remains: Under what conditions does spontaneous, lighthearted play become intensely serious competitive play? And what does the transition from spontaneous natural play to structured sporting events bound by arbitrary rules tell us about human nature?

In some way, human aggression would seem to account for the paradoxical movement from play as free-spirited "fun" to highly controlled and competitive athletic games. After all, aggression is the human energy with which we must test the waters of life into which we are plunged *willy-nilly*. We had no prior choice of whether to exist or not. Now that we do exist, we have limited choices over the conduct of our lives and no say whatever regarding our ultimate and inevitable demise. If we are challenged by the great game of life, then the contest seems *not* to be played on a *level field*. Nature always wins out in the end. Perhaps it is here that human aggression asserts itself with ingenious initiative, creating a challenge—a contest—of its own. Human beings want to face challenges based on rules which they themselves make. In devising formal sporting games with rules that we all agree to follow, we are playing out the myth of Sisyphus. We are going to play the game on our terms— not on Zeus's terms. Perhaps we cannot control the ultimate game of life, but we have a lot to say about the humanly contrived contests that take place between designated boundaries and are governed by rules of our own making. In athletic competitions, human beings establish their own standards of winners and losers, which seem much more equitable than what life offers. While nature dooms us to an irreversible termination of life, those who are *vanquished* on the human playing field can come back to try again. There is always the next game. There is always next year. Sport is not a *metaphor* of life; it is a temporary *alternative* to life—a life played out on our terms. It is an opportunity to experience a sense of accomplishment and purpose with the outcome entirely in human hands. Athletic contests are an expression of human freedom and hope—freedom to live (while playing) according to self-imposed rules and hope that the next event will bring success and victory. In creating their own competition through athletic events, human beings are challenging nature by asserting their independence to do something apart from the inevitable forces that surround them. Jean Paul Sartre (1905–1980) expresses the significance of human freedom through the spirit of play:

> What is play indeed if not an activity of which man is the first origin, for which man himself sets the rules and which has no consequences except according to the rules posted? As soon as man apprehends himself as free and wishes to use his freedom, a freedom, by the way, which could just as well be anguish, then his activity is play. The first principle of play is man himself; through it *he escapes his natural nature;* he himself sets the value and the rules for his acts and consents to

play only according to the rules which he himself
has established and defined.

This expression of human freedom and independence through games of competition does not resolve the human paradox of desiring both care-free play and serious sports. Paradoxes, after all, are not "resolved"; they are confronted and acknowledged. Human beings bring all their puzzling confusion into the athletic arena. Athletic contests reveal an enigmatic mix of frivolous fun and intense gravity, to play for the sake of playing ("It matters not if you win or lose. It's how you play the game.") and to play with the ferocious intent to succeed ("Winning is not the most important thing— it is the *only* thing."). Put in proper context, however, athletic competitions are not merely about playing, nor merely about winning. They are human expressions of freedom and a defiant creation of arbitrary rules of a game that postpones the inevitable "victory" of nature.

All cultures throughout history have expressed this human desire to engineer some control of life through competitive games. Early in human history, the events are ritualistic—performed to please the gods who would hopefully temper the forces of nature, but enjoyed nonetheless by the participants. If human beings are bound to compete in a losing cause with an unforgiving nature and fickle divinities, then why not create a *contest* of their own with rules and outcomes in human hands? It may not meliorate the ultimate struggle with nature, but at least the competition will be a fair contest planned, performed, and judged by human beings.

Ancient Greek society called the place of contest, *Agon*. Perhaps it was the gymnasium or the race course or fields for javelin and discus events. The term became identified with the contest itself, and was used for all sorts of competitive events, including oratorical contests in the law courts and the highly valued contest to determine the best tragedian in Athens. It was the *Agon* of athletic competitions, however, that was most celebrated as the blood, sweat, and tears of aggressive competition. All of the extant odes of the poet Pindar sing the praises of the victorious athletes in the Pan-Hellenic games— those *Agonistic* trials of strength, skill, and stamina that brought fame and honor to the winners. It is not merely ironic that games—events designed for enjoyment and recreation -- are pitched to a level of competitiveness that engenders sheer agony. The motto of television's popular *Wide World of Sports* had it half right: "The thrill of Victory and the Agony of Defeat." However, for victors and vanquished alike, *agony* is the price of competitive athletic contests—an agony that the participants find highly enjoyable.

The term *Agon also* suggests fiercely competitive contests involving a life-death struggle, as was the military *Agon* against the Persians on the plains of Marathon or at the Pass at Thermopylae. War is often likened to a sporting contest, but metaphorical language aside, war is no game. The ultimate aggression of human beings aimed at eradicating each other results in an *agony* unknown in any athletic competition. Like Sisyphus, we challenge nature by creating our own contests of sport through the spirit of play, but in warfare, we hasten nature's work and destroy each other prematurely with severe cruelty. Perhaps we have more to fear from each other than from the gods or nature. Athletic games would seem to serve the purpose of channeling all the ferocity of aggression manifested in warfare into the competition of sports. Human aggression is transferred from the deadly battlefield of war to the more benign playing field of sports. The progression suggested here is that of first establishing competitive games as a defiant challenge to the gods and nature whose unfair "rules" are beyond human control. The next enlightened step is the realization that human aggression in warfare is more quick and cruel than what nature has in store for us. If we—not nature—are to be our own worst enemies, then why not feign an enmity on the field of competitive sports where winners are celebrated and losers are not mourned?

Epilogue

What does it all mean? Life? Life on planet Earth? Being human? What does it mean to be temporal, to exist in time—a passage through a series of "nows" that leaves behind a dead past and moves toward a future that is never present? If all of our knowledge is bound to immediate experiences, then can we only infer about the future in terms of what is, at best, probable? Is absolute knowledge beyond the reckoning of our limited cognitive abilities? Are the absolute ideals of our value system comparable to the notion of infinity in math and science—approached but never attained? Temporality implies that human existence is developmental. We start humbly as one-celled inviable zygotes and rapidly develop into highly complex organisms. Is there any stage of development that is more important than others? Is "adulthood" the crowning glory of human existence—to reach the "age of reason" and move beyond—to where?

What does it mean to be "self-aware"? To identify with an "I" that establishes a unique personal identity, which alone is the only *direct* and *immediate* certitude that we have of anything? How can we be singular individuals and members of a social order at the same time? How can we determine where one's rights as an individual end and the rights of a collective begin? How can we be so certain of our individual importance when our time here is so fleeting and so quickly forgotten? Are we, human beings, anomalies of nature? All of nature seems pre-determined to act with exact causal efficacy—nonliving things by a natural necessity, living things by organic or instinctive necessity. We say we are free. Are we really? Do we stand in marked contrast to all of nature and defy the determined laws that inextricably bind all things to the earth and the universe? What do we make of the acute awareness of our own personal identity? We were not born knowing who we are as individuals. When did each person come to the realization that "I am who I am and not someone else"? Are these relevant questions, or merely nonsense interrogations of someone who thinks too much? Might we just as well ask, "How fast can numbers fly?" and expect the same quizzical and patronizing look as when asking some of the previous questions? But can we ever "think too much"? What would it say of the human species if we stopped "thinking" and became docile to the molding forces of social customs that resist any attempt to change?

The ancient Greeks perceived the enigma that was woven into the fabric of being human. They surmised that humanity was sort of stuck in a halfway house between the gods and the animals. Human beings were smart enough to ask all the questions but too dumb to have all the answers. Members of the human species, in a sense, were players in a continuous tragedy of constantly facing tantalizing puzzles, the answers to which were always a bit beyond their reach. And yet these people of a unique era did seem to accomplish an amazing number of feats, among which was the representation of life's tragedy on the stage. But tragedy, for the Greeks who set the standard for staged drama, was simply the other face of comedy. When we can laugh at the incongruity of life, is that more than a mere psychological defense mechanism that temporarily avoids the tragedy? Staged comedy capitalizes on the incongruous. The slapstick comedian attired in formal evening wear with top hat, silk scarf and tails, slips on a banana peel and lands on his keister. This undignified end is so incongruous to the dress and intentions of the person. Do we laugh or cry? If zany slapstick humor is at the one end of the spectrum, then perhaps the ultimate incongruity of tragic-comedy is at the other end. We long for immortality, we want to live forever, and yet we know we will perish. Perhaps if we can laugh at that incongruity, we can laugh at anything. And of course we do. The dark humor of death is subject of many comic jokes and routines. Is life basically about laughing and crying and knowing when it is proper to do one or the other?

Many authors of significant fame claim that these human puzzles can be framed in terms of baseball as metaphor, that baseball is much more than it appears to be. It is more than a game. It is a symbolic field of dreams where heroes return from beyond and either receive or bequeath redemption. Some attribute a magical realism to the game and envision special players as knights seeking the Holy Grail and even bringing thunder and lightning from the sky in their quest. Many have equated baseball to religion, liking players to saints and sinners, memorabilia to relics, ball parks to cathedrals, and the baseball hall of fame to the Holy of Holies itself. Many worshippers of the game make it a life-long goal to visit every baseball stadium in the country and to complete the pilgrimage with a visit to Cooperstown. Under this religious conceit, Abner Doubleday is dubbed as either creator or prophet —either would be off the mark since scholars have debunked Doubleday as being the inventor of the game. Regardless, it is of interest to see a kid's game offered as bigger-than-life symbols of supernatural answers to life's ultimate questions. Questions that were posed above.

Did the boys of the Sixth Avenue Wildcats find the answers to life's tragic and comic questions by playing the game of baseball? Was Reds a prophet leading the boys out of the wilderness of pubescence? If so, he was not recognized as such by a greater society. At least, not by anyone untouched by the words of his story. How about the other boys? Were they mythic models of adolescent youngsters navigating the perilous straits between Scylla and Charybdis, riding the perilous narrows between childhood and adulthood? Or were they just kids playing a game?

Perhaps it is a distortion of reality to present baseball as the ultimate metaphor to God and the Promised Land. Billy never claimed that the one and only homer he hit was directed by the Hammer of Thor. It never would have occurred to him to make such a claim. The boys knew they used bats at the plate, not thunder sticks. Ernie never thanked Vulcan when he threw out runners attempting to steal a base. He had a good arm. Reds never thought that he led the team by some kind of divine right. Reds had a calm demeanor and reassuring mannerisms that commanded respect in much the same way that a successful actor has stage presence. To make the game bigger than what it is by assigning mythological or theological meaning to the game is to make baseball something it is not. The heroes of mythology were proto-theologians trying to pacify those aspects of nature they could neither understand nor control. Many of the heroes and their problems would be washed away by the incoming tide of scientific discoveries.

This is not to take any literary merit away from those accounts of baseball as the road to God. It is simply to say that baseball as mythic or divine is not the boys' story. They did not play that kind of game. Theirs is a real story of kids playing a game that is not controlled by gods, heroes, or adults. They never reached big league fame either in real life or in fiction. No one will ever know their story because it is too mundane for a world that wants demigods on the field and intervening gods from afar. They played a real game that was played on their terms in their way, and they did not care if anyone knew about it. The profound questions and paradoxes of life *could be* intertwined with their adventures on that cow-pasture field on which they played, but that was not for them to say. If they laughed and cried at the sweet and bitter innings of their game, it was because they did not distinguish sufficiently between playing at baseball and playing at life. Taking hiking trips, going to school, attending the movie theater, studying their received religious faith, playing with their pets, attending funerals with their parents, learning about democracy, being infatuated with girls—and yes, playing baseball. That was their ordinary life. They would never make the bestseller's list of magical or divine baseball stories. Neither would most ordinary people. They intuitively knew, however, that baseball *and* life were only a game—but it was their game. It was their life.

About the Author

J oseph Romano is professor emeritus of philosophy at Cabrini University in Radnor, Pennsylvania. He continues to teach and advise in a limited role.

He earned his doctorate degree from Bryn Mawr College and was the recipient of two post-doctoral grants from the Carnegie Foundation. He also was granted a visiting professorship at the University of Louvain in Belgium. He enjoys writing about the philosophy of real ordinary lived-experiences. He co-authored a course on "Baseball and the American Tradition." He lives with his wife, Jeanne, in Malvern, Pennsylvania. He has two daughters and four grandchildren.